THE WICCA COOKBOOK

THE WICCA
COOKBOOK

Recipes, Ritual, and Lore

JAMIE WOOD AND TARA SEEFELDT

SECOND EDITION

CELESTIAL ARTS
Berkeley

Published in the United States by Celestial Arts, an
imprint of the Crown Publishing Group, a division of
Random House, Inc., New York.
www.crownpublishing.com
www.tenspeed.com

Celestial Arts and the Celestial Arts colophon are
registered trademarks of Random House, Inc.

Library of Congress Cataloging-in-Publication Data
Wood, Jamie.
  The Wicca cookbook : recipes, rituals, and lore /
Jamie Wood and Tara Seefeldt. — 2nd ed.
      p. cm.
  Includes bibliographical references (2nd ed.) and index.
  1. Wicca. 2. Cooking—Religious aspects—Wicca.
3. Religious calendars—Wicca. 4. Sabbat. I. Seefeldt,
Tara. II. Title.
  BP605.W53W66 2010
  641.5—dc22
                                2010028309

ISBN 978-1-58761-104-9

Second edition

Printed in the United States
Design by Jeff Puda

10 9 8 7 6 5 4 3 2 1

ACKNOWLEDGMENTS

I would like to thank the Mother for all Her guidance during the process of writing this book and revising it for the second edition. Special thanks to my kids Alethia, Skyler, and Kobe for always being an inspiration. Thank you to my agent Julie Castiglia who believed I could write a book even before I knew I could. I adore you. My gratitude goes out to my editor, Veronica "Fuzzy" Randall, with whom I have much fun and mischief. I am grateful for the scary and fun experiences since the first edition of this book; they have made me stronger, more confident, and thank the stars, better able to take a joke. So, while I don't fly around on brooms, own thirteen black cats, or have warts on my chin, I do cackle from time to time, believe in the magic of night, the power of dreams, and the love that connects us all.

Bright blessings,

Jamie Wood

I am deeply grateful for the friendship and support of all of those who donated recipes.

High on this list is Terrie Hurt. Her good humor, depth of knowledge, and generous support was amazing and went above and beyond. I especially want to thank my dear friends Dawna Perry and Andy Honker for bravely offering themselves up as taste testers for several recipes. They offered advice and feedback that was invaluable. I would like to thank Beth Luey for her advice, patience, and great sense of humor. I would like to thank my family members who listened patiently to endless discussions about the project. Lastly, of course, I thank my husband, Doug, for being truly himself, a wonderful life partner who has provided unending support, advice, and encouragement in this and all things.

Blessed be,

Tara Seefeldt

CONTENTS

INTRODUCTION

According to ancient earth-based traditions, a deep-seated spirituality has always been a part of food preparation. When cooking is combined with a ceremonial significance, it transforms an ordinary task into an extraordinary connection with the Divine Source. Without requiring any commitment to Wicca and its beliefs, *The Wicca Cookbook* offers ways to celebrate and honor the divinity in nature and each of us.

Wicca, also known as Witchcraft, the Craft, or simply the Old Religion, is a nature-based religion, close in ideology to Native American and shamanistic traditions. As an earth-centered religion, its origins predate Judaism, Christianity, Islam, Buddhism, and Hinduism. Wicca comes from the Saxon root *wicce*, loosely translated as "wise" or "to bend or shape the unseen forces." The knowledge of Wicca is derived from the movement of the sun, moon, and stars, and the cycles of the seasons.

No hard and fast rules exist in Wicca. It is not based on a degree or a set of beliefs but rather on a practice of aligning oneself with the natural forces of life. Wiccans honor and celebrate the female energy known as the Goddess in Her triple reflection of the Maiden, Mother, and Crone. Her Consort, the male energy known as the God, Hunter, or Horned One, completes the total being of the Divine Source. Emphasis is placed on personal experience and a tolerance of other paths and lifeways. Wiccans recognize the innate presence of divinity in the natural world, each individual, and the cycle of the seasons.

Within Wicca are eight sabbats, each holding a sacrosanct place on the Great Solar Wheel of the Year, also known as the Mandala of Nature. The sabbats give way to each other like the changing of the seasons. Each sabbat is celebrated with corresponding symbols, traditional foods, herbs, and the ritual invocation of Divine power through the creation of sacred space.

The Wicca Cookbook is divided into these nature-based festivals. Each recipe is preceded with a hallowed meaning, the ingredients' therapeutic value, historical significance, or a spell or ritual that you can perform in conjunction with the food preparation. Great value is placed on personal creativity, poetry, and the artful integration of different myths and ritual elements. Therefore, you are encouraged to add to or create a ceremony or meditation that reflects your feelings and understanding.

The recipes include many edible flowers and medicinal herbs, whose use dates back to the Middle Ages and even earlier, when ancient people included them in recipes as well as used them for their healing and medicinal properties. Except for those few that were grown locally, most herbs were quite costly in the Middle Ages and protected with tenacity. Only the lady of the household held the key to the herb cabinet, since the servants were not to be trusted with such a precious commodity. The village midwife held the secrets to the curative uses of the flowers and herbs and the lore was then passed down through the generations.

Meals were heavily spiced to add flavor to otherwise bland food and in an attempt to cover up the unsavory taste of decaying food. Flowers and herbs were also used in dishes to impart both flavor and beneficial medicinal effects. The fragrances and textures of herbs and flowers delighted the senses. Their importance can be seen in the many treatises on gardening that have survived from the Middle Ages. Eighty-six plants are listed in a fifteenth-century treatise on gardening, and the author clearly indicates that he could have added more. Herbs have long been considered essential for a full and happy life.

Each flower and herb possesses unique characteristics that not only enhance the flavor but also add a sacred quality that imparts the Divine in every dish. By inviting Mother Nature into your dishes, you welcome the flow of Divine spirituality. In this cookbook, herbs and flowers from the Mother's garden are used in recipes during sabbats that coincide with their seasonal peak. This alignment increases the spiritual benefit of the recipe and reflects the Universe's perfect rhythm. Eating foods at their prescribed times not only offers more nutrients, it also ensures heightened medicinal potency.

You may either grow your own herbs and edible flowers or purchase them. A delightful kitchen herb garden conveys the message of Divine abundance. It reminds one of the wealth that is available to us all in the natural world.

The recipes in *The Wicca Cookbook* call for fresh herbs, but in most cases you may substitute dried ones. When substituting dried herbs for fresh ones, halve the required measurement of fresh herbs to get the desired amount of herbs. You may even choose to grow your own herbs and dry them for your culinary purposes. (See Growing and Using Herbs, beginning on page 23, for suggestions on harvesting, drying, and preserving herbs.) If you do not have the time or means to cultivate your own garden, you can obtain medicinal herbs from various seed and nursery companies that specialize in growing herbs. In addition, we encourage you to grow flowers specifically for culinary purposes. If this is not possible, be sure to purchase flowers that are organically grown and free of pesticides.

Cook with as many whole foods as you can obtain. The way in which you create the recipes will reflect your personal spirituality and love. This individuality is vitally important in Wicca. So create and enjoy! Wicca adores and praises our uniqueness. The Old Religion revels in individualism, recognizing that every one of us is a perfect child of the Universe and created from the same Divine Source. This Divinity is both male and female; however, to reestablish our connection with the earth and the Mother energy and since the feminine power is considered the beginning of all creation, the place from which all life originates, Wiccans often say Mother or Goddess when referring to the Divine Source. We always remain a part of that source, just as the rays of sunshine never leave the sun. "We have not left that Source to enter a body and die," explains *A Course in Miracles*. We are a life, a spirit having a body for a time, not a body having a life. As such, we each have something miraculous and Divine to offer. Today too many people do not recognize the Divine in everything and everyone. They only see the Divine in extraordinary events, miracles not to be expected every day, whereas Wiccans know magic is commonplace and happens throughout the natural world, manifesting in the smallest acts from hour to hour, day to day, season to season.

Wiccans take part in ceremonies and rituals as a means of performing white magic for healing purposes. White magic is positive and used only to promote good and healing. The innate good within Wiccan magic transforms negativity, allowing the old to die and make room for the new. The cyclical change of the seasons in nature and human life is seen as the essential erotic dance of life, death, and rebirth. New growth comes from death and destruction of old ideas, past pain, and bad habits, just as the greenest plants grow best from a pile of compost.

Each ceremony is as unique as the Wiccan performing it. Some ritual items are common to almost every Wiccan tradition, such as the *athame* (ritual knife) and *chalice* (ritual cup). Other tools that you may want to incorporate into your realm of magic could include bells, a Book of Shadows (a secret diary of spells, rituals, or dreams), a *besom* (broom), a *burin* (engraving tool), candles, cauldrons, cords, crystals, drums, incense, jewelry, special plates, pentacles, rattles, rune stones, scourges, statues, swords, staves, tarot cards, and wands. But it will be your own personality that adds a unique dimension to each magical incantation, providing the meaning and resonance. The tools just enhance the process and help you focus.

The key to building power within your tools and manifesting that which you desire is to use your ritual items often. These tools will help you connect with the Mother when you are feeling detached and alone. Place them where you see them every day. Many Wiccans choose to create an altar where they can arrange their most sacred items. An altar offers a refuge for meditation, relaxation, and observance. You can also place your ritual items throughout the house, reminding you at every turn that the Mother is waiting to shower you with her love and guidance. With regular use, your tools will soon be charged with your unmatched energy and ready for the next ritual.

When you perform rituals, you will be invoking sacredness into being. Whether you are holding ritual ceremonies, casting spells, or working with symbols, always keep a positive goal in mind. One commonly held Wiccan belief is the threefold law: Whatever you do comes back to you three times. The first rule of all Wiccan traditions is "Harm to None." Wicca is truly a joyous religion with a reverence for the benevolent Divine Source who gives lovingly in abundance.

Rituals remind us of the deep spirituality found in everyday life as well as in sacred ceremony. Rituals recognize and honor the moon, the sun, the Goddess, the God, the sabbats, and more. They offer guidelines for honoring the changing seasons, planetary cycles, and the Mother. All Wiccan rituals welcome a personal touch as each practitioner contemplates the higher power within and surrounding them. Through rituals, Wiccans work magic that takes them beyond the human limitations of mind and substance, creating a sacred connection with Spirit.

This is not to say one must deny or disregard desires of the flesh. Spell casting for material gain or comfort is a legitimate manifestation of the Divine. We are put here on this earth plane to learn lessons of the highest order such as forgiveness, trust, and the gift of life, but we must still thrive on the material level. When we prosper and flourish, we illustrate to the world the many forms of abundance available to us all. As the faery saying goes, "Work for yourself, and soon you will see that Self is everywhere." By casting a spell, we tell the Universe it is okay to send us our most fervent desires. We will it to happen, and as long as it is in the highest good of all concerned, the Universe complies. We are in charge of our own destiny; we create our own reality. When we look deep within, we see that the Divine Universe is not outside of ourselves, but within us. This revelation is so profound and expansive that Wiccans utilize rituals and symbols to conceive its vastness. It is when you stop trying to understand through the commonplace and the five senses that these rituals and symbols open up those channels of understanding and propel you toward enlightenment and personal growth.

Symbols speak volumes to our unconscious mind of things that cannot be explained, defined, or fully comprehended with our everyday language. They represent concepts that extend far beyond human understanding.

Wiccan symbols provide a point of reference, a wider awareness for "that-which-cannot-be-told," and allow infinite interpretations of experience, especially those in which one feels the connectedness to Spirit. Symbols speak of love and the universal and eternal intelligence that is omnipotent, omniscient, and omnipresent. Symbols put us in touch with our younger selves, when we never doubted out intimate relationship with the Universe. Therefore, they are essential for recognizing and remembering the love the Mother holds for all Her children.

Symbols hold a place in magical history as well. Often symbols were used to hide the workings of ancient people from a populace afraid of self-sufficient women. Many people had moved so far away from their natural roots that they deemed women who practiced the Old Religion evil witches. The pentagram, ankh, and symbols of the Goddess and the moon in Her many phases were carved into woodworking, sewn onto robes, or engraved onto chalices and athames. These symbols provided identification amongst fellow worshipers, which enabled them to maintain anonymity from the society at large.

You need not belong to a coven of witches to practice these age-old traditions: you just need to believe that something wiser and older than you is working in harmony with nature. Through heightened consciousness—seeing the life force in everything—you can direct nature's gifts for your highest good as well as for that of others.

To ensure the most potent kitchen magic, we suggest that you consecrate your kitchen, stove, and utensils. Consecrating your tools is a means of purifying them from past energies and intent and infusing them with your vibrations and purpose. If this ritual seems complicated, we invite you to create your own for manifesting a sacred environment that feels right for you.

Place a pentacle on your kitchen counter. A pentacle is a physical representation of the pentagram, a five-pointed star, which symbolizes the four elements in balance with Spirit. Fill a chalice or other cup with water. The chalice is symbolic of the receptive passivity of the Mother's womb. With your finger or an athame, draw three pentagrams in the air over the chalice and say

> *I purify thee, O Element of Water,*
> *And cast out from thee*
> *All impurities and negativity.*
> *By My Will so Mote it Be.*

Place a pinch of salt on the pentacle. Draw three pentagrams over the salt and say

> *I purify thee,*
> *O Element of Salt,*
> *Free of contamination, pure by nature,*
> *I infuse my blessing upon thee.*
> *By My Will so Mote it Be.*

Add the salt to the water and say

> *I mix this water and salt*
> *So that whatever it touches*
> *Shall be blessed by my pure intent.*
> *By My Will so Mote it Be.*

Walk around the perimeter of your kitchen and sprinkle the stove, oven, your utensils, and anything else you wish to be purified. Say

> *By casing this water and salt*
> *No interference can permeate*
> *My spells good and true.*
> *By My Will so Mote it Be.*

Place an inch of sand in a thurible or other safe incense burner. Burn charcoal, a representation of the element of fire, on top of the sand. You may substitute a lit candle for the charcoal and use stick incense as well. Draw three pentagrams over the charcoal and say

> *I purify thee, O Element of Fire,*
> *Free of contamination, pure by nature,*
> *I infuse my blessing upon thee.*
> *By My Will so Mote it Be.*

Place incense, symbol of air, on the pentacle. Draw three pentagrams over the incense and say

> *I purify thee, O Element of Air,*
> *And cast out from thee*
> *All impurities and negativity.*
> *By My Will so Mote it Be.*

Add some incense to the coals and say

> *I mix this fire and air*
> *So that whatever it touches*
> *Shall be blessed by my pure intent.*
> *By My Will so Mote it Be.*

You are now ready to begin cooking. When preparing your dishes, it is important to remember the sacredness of food preparation. There are two joys to gain from creative cooking within a hallowed space: one, in which you are cocreator with the Mother, thus allowing Divine interpretation to shine through you; and the second, in which you welcome the creative forces, enabling all Her love to flow from Her through your hands and kitchen to your loved ones.

When you cook, declare yourself an artist at work. Handle each ingredient with loving care. See the life force still pulsing through each whole food. Allow your ego to step aside and make room for divination and magic to take place. When you are creating with the Mother, you may find that inspiration will direct you one way or another; always follow Her instruction. With these recipes, you are creating from the fruits gleaned from the Goddess's garden. Together you bring into being the food that turns into energy for the ones you love.

Making food with love and harmony raises the vibration of the ingredients, invoking their most innate healing powers. Cook not only to satisfy hunger, but also to quench the thirsty soul that is searching for comfort. This process appeases and fulfills the ancient need to intertwine food, security, and love. When a great work of art is completed and the meal is well received by all, remind yourself that you were just present during its creation. Only by working with the Divine and allowing sacred guidance to direct you were you able to create such a masterpiece.

CREATING A SACRED SPACE

Directing positive, calming energy into food preparation begins with the creation of a sacred space. You can choose to make up your own meditations or try this centering ceremony: Stand or sit still. Clear your mind of all thoughts. Envision a silver cord beginning from the center of your solar plexus/stomach and going down through you into Mother Earth. See the cord extend to Her depths. Feel Her strength empower you. Feel the warmth and love surge up that silver cord to your toes, to every outstretched finger, and tingle the top of your head. When you feel centered, begin cooking. As you mix the ingredients, you add a part of yourself with your thoughts and prayers.

Take the time to make your kitchen a loving, welcoming space. If you direct warm and caring energy into your kitchen, others will feel comfortable, and you will feel energized. It is here where you can create magic. Even without a formal ritual, you are still creating positive energy and divination each time you cook with love in your heart.

The most important ingredient you can add to any dish is your intent. All of these recipes can and most likely will be altered to match your personal palate as well as those of your family and friends. The combination of food and spices won't work the magic that your pure intent will.

Centering yourself and making the connection with the Goddess often begins the process of setting up a circle. A circle is usually cast outdoors and provides a place of safety and protection for its participants. We offer the following example of creating a circle, although as you progress along your uniquely inspired Wiccan path you will come across many variations. The important thing is to keep an open mind and incorporate your style and set of beliefs. To cast a circle, you must first ground yourself. Begin by closing your eyes and visualize energy from the Mother rising from the earth, coursing as white light through your entire being. Take three deep breaths. Light dried sage leaves (typically contained in an abalone shell). Direct the smoke all around you, paying close attention to those areas in your aura that feel particularly vulnerable. Pass the sage clockwise around the circle so that your guests can ground themselves with the cleansing herb. To garner protection and guidance from the four directions, hold the sage up to the eastern sky and say

> *Hail all ye Guardians, Guides and Spirits of the East!*
> *We do summon, invoke, and call you forth*
> *That you may bear witness to this ceremony.*
> *Granting your protecting and guidance.*

Move to the south and repeat the chant substituting the proper direction. Repeat this rite for the western and northern quadrants. Then walk clockwise around the circle, sprinkle grain as an offering for the God, pour wine or fruit juice on the earth for the Goddess, and say

> *By these offerings to the God and Goddess,*
> *We ask for the inspiration and direction from*
> *Both the feminine and masculine aspects of Deity.*
> *We declare this circle has been cast.*
> *Between all worlds we stand,*
> *To create magic with intent good and pure.*
> *By Our Will so Mote it Be!*

When you cast a circle, you create a space that exists between worlds, such as the physical and spiritual or human and faery. Once you have called in the spirits and guardians of the four directions and elements and made offerings to Goddess and God, you have created a clearing where powers cross and meet and linear time no longer exists. Just like Christians go to a church and Jews go to a temple, Wiccans turn to Mother Earth, and it is upon her life-giving soil that they worship, pray, and perform rituals.

Before you walk away from any ritual in which you have cast a circle, you must close that circle. When you draw a circle and perform magic in its boundaries, you are creating a vortex, or opening, for the spirit world. This is a sacred space that needs to be protected and honored so that the intentions you put forth in that arena will stay intact and pure. Therefore, it is imperative that circle be closed. Begin by thanking all of the deities, guardians, and angels for coming and lending their support and guidance. Walk three times counterclockwise around your circle to neutralize the energy you raised and say

> By my will I erase thee,
> O circle of power.
> Return to Mother Earth
> Once more to the ground.
> By My Will so Mote it Be!

Then brush away the threshold at the eastern door. From the outside, brush away the image of the circle.

As we work to achieve and maintain a spiritual connection that is in harmony with nature and the Goddess, we first use different props, which provide the medium through which we tap into the available energy. Some readers have become so proficient in connecting with Spirit that they do not need this ritualistic form of setting a circle. On their spiritual quest and way to enlightenment, some Wiccans have become more aware and present and live in the now moment. Spell casting has developed into a natural appendage of their Wiccan path. Like actors rehearsing for a Broadway show—where markings are set for positions and cues are given—after enough practice, their spiritual course and alignment with Spirit becomes uncontrived and flows with an easy rhythm. We applaud these solitary Wiccans.

We remind you to spiral down to the physical level after working with Spirit. When channeling and meditating with the Goddess, some will feel cold or warm but definitely otherworldly in that quiet, sacred space between two worlds. Like the discomfort of being jolted awake from a lovely dream, a quick return to the earthly plane can be painful and some-times frightening. It is a sudden disconnection from the Mother that causes this lost, empty feeling. We implore that after you work with the Goddess, you gently return yourself to the mundane level either by meditation, move-ment, or water. Water is fluid like the Goddess and can remind you of the connection you felt. It will ease you back to the denser experience of the physical world.

SPELL CASTING

ithin this book several methods for rituals and spell casting are offered. Before you decide to cast a spell, you need to ask yourself the following four questions:

1. IS THE SPELL NECESSARY?

Have you done all that you can on the mundane level to manifest this goal? In other words, wouldn't it be easier to just sweep the floor than to spend the energy trying to cast a spell to make the broom sweep on its own accord? Sometimes people cast spells to rid themselves of a problem because they don't think they can meet the challenge and are afraid of failure. They do not pay attention to the lesson Spirit is offering. The Goddess often has a higher opinion of us than we do. She places obstacles in our way to give us the opportunity to test our tools and to realize how capable and strong we are. If we allow ourselves to learn from our mistakes, we will find treasures in our soul. We will awaken to the realization that we are a part of Spirit and in possession of all the goodness and courage that exists within the Divine. With this intimate experience and the discovery of your new abilities, you will feel empowered.

2. WILL IT SERVE YOUR HIGHEST GOOD?

Is it what you really need? You want to manifest the essence (peace, harmony, joy, or love that can be found in a home) versus the thing (the blue with white trim, two-story colonial house). We often get caught up in the belief that only a particular form will make us happy. After casting a spell, we are often surprised when the exact house, partner, or car either does not present itself, or worse, does appear but does not bring us the quality of life we were after. Wouldn't it be easier if we distilled our desires to their basic essence and began with this focus in mind? Visualize what it will feel like, not what it will look like, when your spell has come to fruition. In your spell casting, be specific about your aspirations, not the method used to accomplish the goal or its appearance. Express the need, ask for the desire, and allow the Divine to give you its interpretation of your needs. It is a good idea to end the spell by saying "This or something better." Release your attachment to the outcome. This is not about your ego and ability to manifest whatever you feel like but about living a life in harmony with nature.

3. WILL IT HARM ANYONE, INCLUDING YOURSELF?

Sometimes it is necessary for you to feel hurt before a need can be met. It may hurt to learn that you are being selfish, but when you peel away layers of unhelpful aspects of yourself, your life will be better and more fulfilled. We are all connected, and spells that have a positive rippling effect and benefit others will manifest much more smoothly. Hurting is a momentary pain, whereas harming another causes irreparable and long-term damage. It may hurt to have a broken bone set, but if it isn't, it will not heal properly. To harm violates the first rule of the Craft, "Harm to None." The energy we send out returns to us through our earthly brothers and sisters. In addition to the negative karma you will accrue, harming another is not acceptable in Wicca.

4. ARE YOU WILLING TO OWN THE RESPONSIBILITIES OF THE RESULTS?

If the answer is not a resounding "Yes!" then don't do it. If there is the slightest doubt as to whether or not a spell should be cast, then it should not be done. Once you have directed your will and set your intentions, a myriad of outcomes can manifest. You must be willing to accept however the events unfold, for this is not in your power to determine. The outcome will be a Divine representation of the Goddess's will: "Not my will but Thine be done." Often Spirit knows better what we need and can present our needs and desires in a much better package than we imagine. Spirit's knowledge is limitless. It contains all possibilities. We are restricted to conceiving only what we have experienced or to what we have been exposed. Spirit does not have these boundaries.

After you have considered these points and weighed your answers carefully, it is important that you make an appropriate offering before you cast a spell. An offering, or sacrifice, as it is also called, completes the cycle of the give-and-take that is so apparent in nature. It is not necessary to make a sacrifice for spells of self-protection, connection to angels, guides, or deities, or the access to tools and abilities needed to meet such basic needs as food, shelter, clothing, and health. These are your Divine rights.

Sacrifices can take all forms and shapes. A sacrifice is what you intend to offer in exchange for what you want to receive. Your offer may involve donating time or money, planting a tree, or going without chocolate or caffeine. Determine the appropriate sacrifice by intuition, omens, which often appear in nature, or divination. Ask the Goddess for a sign of the appropriate offering and remain observant. There are several ways to divine a sacrifice, from casting stones to using a crystal pendulum. Whichever way feels best for you and resonates with your beliefs is always the best way for you to divine.

Our power comes from the Goddess. We exist in the Divine, and the Divine lives in us. We are a product of our own making. By casting spells, we tap into the nebulous waiting energy and bring it into form, much like turning on a light and utilizing the available electricity. It is our responsibility to access and use that energy for good in and by love.

Your harmonious connection to the Divine will lead you to live in peace with the ebbing and flowing rhythms of ever-changing nature, just as our ancestors did.

MEDIEVAL COOKING

Throughout *The Wicca Cookbook*, we refer to recipes, way of life, and customs of the Middle Ages, also known as medieval times. The Middle Ages was a transitional time when the Old Ways were slipping into disuse and going underground as Christianity rose in power and popularity. Still, the old and the new ways coexisted. The patriarchal religions had not completely gained control over the hearts and minds of the average person. Many people held on strongly to the Old Ways and reverence for the Goddess. Today Wiccans rejoice in the teachings and lore of medieval people who lived attuned to nature. Perhaps through the echoes of these anecdotes and recipes, we can learn valuable ways to draw closer to the Mother.

To learn from the medieval person, we must first come to an understanding of their needs and circumstances. Their history is quite interesting and provides a basis from which many Wiccan traditions are derived.

Cooking in the Middle Ages was quite different from the modern approach most of us utilize today. Medieval people did not have refrigerators or stove-top ranges to help them prepare their food. The appearance of a typical kitchen in the Middle Ages was aptly described by a young cleric named Alexander Neckham who journeyed to Paris in the twelfth century. He noted that most kitchens had a central table where vegetables could be minced, chopped, or otherwise cut up and a cleaning place where domestic fowl could be plucked and cleaned. Common utensils and cooking items found in most homes included pots, tripods, a mortar and pestle, spoons, knives, bowls, a hook, a hatchet, a cauldron, and a griddle. Most homes also had a pickling vat, a pepper mill, and a hand mill for flour.

Linens such as towels and tablecloths hung from a pole in the pantry to keep them away from mice. The larder was stocked with a sauce dish, a saltcellar, candelabras, and baskets. Many homes also had a cellar where the home owner stored casks, wineskins, cups, and basins. Most people kept plenty of drinks on hand. The cellar held the pure wine, cider, beer, unfermented wine, mixed wine, claret, nectar, mead, and "clove-spiced wine for gluttons whose thirst is unquenchable," as Urban Tigner Holmes, Jr., wrote in *Daily Living in the Twelfth Century*.

To avoid infestation by rodents, the house owner might employ a wily tabby cat and her kittens to police the cellar for vermin. Off the cellar, there was using a garderobe (latrine) through which the filth of the kitchen was eliminated. A home owner normally had to hire a day laborer to clean the garderobe, since the house servants objected to that duty!

The oven was the focus of the medieval kitchen. Its management determined the success or failure of the kitchen, not to mention the job of the cook. The fire in the oven had to be closely watched to make sure it was the right temperature and without smoke. While the oven gradually lost its heat, the experienced cook made full use of its warmth. A variety of dishes were cooked throughout the day, taking advantage of the varying intensity of the heat. At the end of the day, often a pear dish or some other dessert would be baked, thereby utilizing the remaining heat in the oven. The medieval cook was a master of time management, not to mention eco-friendly energy efficiency.

Meanwhile, pots were moved around the hearthstone to make good use of the various levels of heat. Sometimes a few coals would be dragged to one side of the hearthstone to create a smaller, cooler fire to keep a prepared dish warm. A spit for roasting was usually turned by hand, most likely by a kitchen maid. Tripods were used at various levels to keep things boiling, simmering, or baking. Normally, the kitchen contained a pothook that could swing over the fire and hold a cauldron. The hook was sometimes attached to a chain that could be lowered or raised.

Spices were kept in a special cupboard in the kitchen. Many medieval cookery books refer to mixtures of spices with particular names. These mixtures were so common that there was no need to explain them. Research has given some clues to what they might have been.

The mixtures were called *powders*. Two of the most common were *powder blanche* or *douce* and *powder fort*. The familiar mixture of apple pie spices (cinnamon, ginger, cloves, nutmeg, and sugar) is probably similar to the powder douce. The fort powder most likely contained pepper, at the very least. Still, there is no real way of knowing, since the mixtures varied from cook to cook, from region to region, and from commercial supplier to supplier. Housewives who did not have a ready supply of spices could buy these mixtures premade from the local merchants.

Edible flowers and herbs were a mainstay of medieval cookery. Common flowers used in a variety of dishes included roses, lilies, heliotrope, violets, mandrake, and peonies. Special care was taken to grow and harvest Mother Nature's bounty. Careful drying and storing of these herbs assured availability throughout the year.

Herbs were vitally important to the medieval cook. Parsley and sage were the easiest herbs to grow and most prevalent. Other herbs common to medieval times included bay, pennyroyal, fennel, coriander, savory, hyssop, mint, rue, dittany, sorrel, basil, dill, marjoram, rocket, absinthe, anise, mustard, and white pepper. As you can see, many of these herbs are found on grocery shelves today.

Medieval people adored spices—the spicier, the better! Ginger, clove, cinnamon, licorice, incense, myrrh, aloe, balsam, scotch bonnet, and cypress were imported from faraway lands. The favored herbs that grew in Europe included saffron, thyme, pennyroyal, and borage.

Pepper was the spice of choice and highly sought after. However, for the less fortunate, mustard seed was substituted, as it grew easily in Europe. Other favorite flavorings of the common folk included onions, garlic, leeks, and chives (all cheap and plentiful). In fact, so much garlic was pounded in the mortar and used that it inspired a saying: "The mortar always smells of garlic."

As with spice mixtures, the instructions for medieval spices depended not on exact measurements as we have today but on the experienced hand

and eye. Medieval people lived their lives relying on this sort of knowledge. The approach to time and measurements was very different from today and tended to be more human and nature based, reflecting the cycles of the moon and the seasons.

As you might assume, the different classes ate different things. Except for the nobles, who had extensive kitchen facilities, most people in the Middle Ages relied mainly on grilling meat over the hearth fire or boiling in a pot. Most homes had large pots, so it is apparent that most meals were stews, soups, and porridges. Stews were made with grains, vegetables, and sometimes meat when available. Other popular processes for cooking and preserving foods included candying, baking, stewing, pickling, and salting.

Favorite vegetables included celery, lettuce, watercress, pumpkins, leeks, onions, shallots, beets, and cabbage. Cabbage, along with coarse bread, was popular among the lower levels of society. Commoners enjoyed fish stews, chicken or rabbit stews, pork and beans, stewed leeks, brussels sprouts, mutton stew, leg of mutton, veal pies, tripe, and cheese tarts or omelets.

Aristocrats ate refined versions of these dishes plus many more, since they could afford a large variety of foods. A nobleman's garden might have contained such delicacies as peaches, lemons, oranges, quinces, pomegranates, almonds, pears, and figs (although some of these might not have grown in the northern countries). Citrus became more available in the later Middle Ages and was consumed mostly by aristocrats. Fruits were delivered to the medieval aristocratic table in cooked form; eating raw produce was considered undignified and only fit for peasant consumption. However, it is difficult to know just how many raw fruits and vegetables were eaten, since the historical sources do not really talk about practices that were commonplace.

Peasants ate meat much less frequently than did aristocrats. Chicken, fish, and eggs were the most affordable source of protein. Since nuts were also a good source of protein, walnuts, filberts (hazelnuts), pistachios, chestnuts, pine nuts, and almonds were all kept on hand in large kitchens.

Many of the smaller varieties of fish were pickled, including mullet, sole, eel mackerel, cod, angler, herring, and oysters. The fish were kept alive in a vivarium, or fish tank or pond, in the kitchen until they were ready to be pickled. The pickling mixture consisted of water mixed with salt.

The foods available in most towns and cities, and to a lesser extent in the countryside, included salad greens, lettuce, cabbage, beans, onions, peas, mushrooms, shallots, watercress, leeks, turnips, rose hips, red apples, melons, pears, aloe berries, pomegranates, plums, nuts, salt meats, fish, wines, flour, and herbs and spices. Medieval Europe even had its own fast food: prepared dishes, breads, and sauces were available for sale in the street markets of most towns and cities. The harried housewife could run to the local merchant and pick up a ready-cooked meat pie if she just could not face cooking that evening.

Other than aristocrats, very few people had ovens in their homes. Countryside villages had communal ovens. Baked bread was made in these communal ovens, with families paying for the use. The bread most people ate was coarse, brown, dark bread, not white bread. White bread was reserved for the nobility, because it was more expensive to produce.

Except in England, where beer or ale was the preferred and safest drink, wine was the drink of choice for all levels of society. Unfortunately, the available water supplies for most town and villages did double duty as well as a latrine. Whenever possible, the smart housewife made sure that her water was drawn upstream from where the sewage entered the stream or river. An interesting feature of many medieval recipes was the call for "pure water," a clear indication that water was often a cause for concern.

The kitchen served many roles for medieval people. In wealthier households, the kitchen served the usual purpose of food preparation, with eating and entertaining being done in the large main room.

Peasants' homes were rarely more than one room. Adults, children, dogs, and even chickens and cows shared the same space. The peasant family sewed, spun, and repaired farm tools in the one room of their dwelling. If they were wealthier peasants and had two rooms, they probably spent a lot of time in the kitchen, since it was usually the warmest room in the house. Then, as now, the kitchen remained the heart of the home. It was favored as a nursery, sewing room, and later for schooling.

For centuries, people have believed that the hearth fire should never go out. If it did, one had to run to the neighbor's house for a piece of charcoal. Otherwise, one could use the fire-striking iron, a two- or three-inch-long piece of iron, which was struck with a piece of flint to cause a spark and light the tinder in the fireplace. Scholars have concluded that, aside from the inconvenience, medieval people did not want the hearth fire to go out for spiritual reasons as well. Ancient people believed that letting the fire extinguish was symbolic of letting the love of the family and home dissipate. This belief fits well with the continuity of love and welcome that surrounds and permeates a Wiccan home.

If keeping a hearth fire is impractical for you, especially for those of you living in desert or tropical climates, you may want to leave a light burning (like a night-light) or always have a candle burning in the window when you are home. This small flame will be a welcoming sight to friends and family.

The medieval world offers a fascinating glimpse into a time when humans lived deep within the cycles of the seasons, closer to the bounty of the earth. It was a time of omens, portents, and signs. Medieval humans lived in a world rich with symbolism and esoteric meaning. The ancient, old ways were giving way to new ways of interacting with and understanding the natural world. In this time of transition and even conflict, our ancestors blended a variety of pagan and Christian beliefs in their daily lives. The process was long and slow. Many people worked to maintain the old ways for numerous years.

We offer the lore and history of this intriguing time so that we can understand where we came from and who we once were. In the not-so-distant past, we lived within the circle of nature. Indeed, *The Wicca Cookbook* honors the past by remembering the Middle Ages and the people of that era. As we turn toward more eco-friendly practices, we are returning to those beliefs and perhaps learning once again to know the natural world and live as one with the Mother.

GROWING AND USING HERBS

rowing your own herbs is a satisfying spiritual act, and what you produce will make your cooking tastier and more appealing!

GROWING AN HERB GARDEN

Whether you plot your herb garden in the kitchen or outdoors, there are many methods and particular techniques to perfecting an abundant and healthy herb garden. Different geographical zones, amount of available sunlight, and the space allotted for gardening all contribute to what you can plant and when you can plant it. Mediterranean herbs such as oregano, thyme, marjoram, and rosemary are great starters for the inexperienced herb grower.

However, there are certain conditions to best ensure your gardening success. The two most important factors in growing herbs are maintaining good drainage and using proper soil. Good drainage is often a direct result of the soil you use. Healthy soil is spongy, aerated, and crumbly. Much can be done to regenerate and improve the condition of your soil. Either perlite or a cactus mix blended with your potting soil will be of great benefit to your plant.

If you choose to grow your herbs in pots, other tricks of the trade for improving the drainage and soil include using a pot that has a drainage hole, placing pots on top of gravel or pebbles, testing the soil's pH balance, composting, and proper watering. Try not to overwater your herbs, as the roots can get moldy. Conversely, do not let your plants get too dry. Terra-cotta pots have a tendency to soak in some of the water, so carefully watch herbs planted in this type of pot.

If you find your herbs have become infested with white fly, aphids, or other pesky insects, try an environmentally sound method that safeguards the health of your plants. Spray your plants with dish soap and let it sit for ten minutes. Spray again with water and wipe the leaves clean.

Although most herbs prefer full sun, some herbs, such as angelica, chervil, ginger, and sweet woodruff grow quite well in the shade. A kitchen window that faces south or has less exposure for at least four to six hours of full sun is best for sun-loving herbs. For the best conditions for growing specific herbs, consult your local nursery or gardening book.

Gardening can be a process of trial and error, and experimentation is often the name of the game. Try growing whatever catches your eye—you might be pleasantly surprised.

Harvesting and Drying Herbs and Flowers

Some believe the best time to harvest most herbs for drying is during summer Solstice, preferably on a sunny, warm day. Rain extracts some of the plant's aromatic oils. Therefore, after a rainstorm wait at least two to three days before harvesting, which will allow the plant time to regain its oils. While all parts of the flower or herb should be picked when dry, distinct parts of the plant are taken at different times of the day.

Leaves should be collected early in the morning, after the dew has evaporated and before the plant flowers. The exception to this rule is evergreen herbs, such as rosemary, which may be harvested throughout the year. Pinching off the leaves instead of cutting them with scissors is recommended when using them for culinary purposes.

Flowers should be harvested midday, when fully opened and at their most majestic beauty. To preserve the health of the plant, practice selective harvesting, only picking one-fourth to one-third of the plant. Treat your collections with great care, making sure not to crush them. Avoid picking herbs and flowers that have been exposed to noxious chemicals or are bruised or damaged. After you've collected them, it is best to place the plants, leaves, and flowers in a flat-bottom basket, English trug, or wooden box until you're prepared to dry them.

After harvesting, try to keep sunlight away from your herb collection. Remove any dirt with light brushing. Wash the herbs only if necessary and gently pat herbs and flowers dry. Too much sun or water affects the quality of the plants, either evaporating or washing away some of the essential oils.

Drying of herbs and flowers should be done as quickly as possible without unduly rushing the process. Choose a dark, well-ventilated room for drying. Maintain a room temperature of 70 to 90°F. Herbs with tender leaves will tend to prefer cooler temperatures, whereas thicker, woodier herbs dry better in warmer temperatures. If you do not have access to a warm attic, a spare room, or the option to naturally dry your herbs outdoors, you can use a heater to dry your herbs. While the herbs dry, it is imperative that you ensure good air circulation, which you can accomplish by opening a window for at least two hours a day.

Smaller leaves, such as sage, rosemary, and lemon balm, should be left on the stem. Gather no more than ten stems loosely together and tie with a string. Hang the bunches upside down with the stems pointing upward. Larger leaves, such as burdock, are best dried individually in a single layer on a screen. Drying is complete when the stems break and the leaves are brittle but do not crumble or turn to powder upon touching them. When dried, rub the leaves off of the stems onto paper and store them in airtight, dry, dark glass or pottery containers. Drying times vary from herb to herb and depend on which part of the plant you are drying. Do not judge whether or not your herbs are dried by comparing them to store-bought herbs. The latter will be darker in color, while yours will have retained more of the plant's natural coloring.

There are two ways to dry flowers. With most flowers, you will need to cut the flower heads from their stems and spread them out on a flat, paper-lined tray. Once they have dried, remove the petals, storing them the same way you would the leaves. Then discard the central portion of the flower. Smaller-headed flowers, such as chamomile and lavender, are dried similarly to herbs hung upside down in bunches with the flowers covered by paper bags.

Some people like to freeze their herbs. We have included two ways to do so. Either cut or pinch off the amount of the herb you wish to freeze and place it in a plastic bag or container. Chill the container until you are ready to use the herb. Alternatively, you can place the cut herbs or flowers in an ice-cube tray, then fill the tray with water. Approximately one teaspoon of herbs or one to two flower heads per ice cube works best. Violets, borage, and pansies come out beautifully and can be used in a punch bowl for a decorative effect. Freezing works well with delicate herbs such as fennel, chives, sweet cicely, and parsley. Basil, dill, coriander, and cilantro don't freeze well and tend to turn brown.

Make sure to label your herbs and flowers. Properly dried flowers and herbs should retain their color and aroma and should last twelve to eighteen months.

Another quick-drying method for preserving herbs and flowers utilizes the oven. Slowly bake the herbs at 150°F until dried. Adjust the temperature in accordance with your oven's particular calibration. Again, look for breakable leaves or petals that do not turn to powder.

MAXIMIZING THE FLAVOR OF DRIED HERBS

While using fresh herbs and flowers is preferred, it is not always possible. Whether you dry your own herbs or buy them, here are a few tips on how to best maximize the taste and therapeutic value of dried herbs and flowers: Smell the herbs before using them to ensure they have maintained their natural aroma. To intensify the flavor, immediately before adding the herbs to other ingredients, rub the herbs in your hands or grind them coarsely in a spice grinder, coffee grinder, or with a mortar and pestle. Using this technique, massage the herbs into meat, poultry, and fish. When combining steamed or boiled vegetables with spices, add melted butter to the herbs. Let the butter and herbs stand for ten minutes before seasoning the vegetables.

Another method used to develop the flavor of herbs calls for soaking dried herbs for several minutes in a liquid that will be used in the recipe, such as stock, water, oil, or juice. To enhance the taste of whole herbs, such as garlic cloves, briefly toast them in a dry, heavy skillet before using. When substituting dried herbs, generally use half of the designated amount of fresh herbs, which comes to approximately one teaspoon of dried herbs per four servings. Remember to taste the food as you progress, adjusting the amount of herbs needed in accordance with your individual preference. One who cultivates a garden walks beside the Mother.

> Springtime comes a'bustling an chattering into view,
> And with Her bringing gifts of greens and everything that's new.
> Summer stretches lazily across the evening sun,
> And settles in a haze of heat when every day is done.
> Then autumn winds begin to stir and once again She tries,
> To paint the trees with brilliance and slowly watch them die.
> In winter there's a hushness, a stillness all around,
> And patiently She waits to spread Her pureness on the ground.
> Often times I wonder at this swift and secret Friend,
> And when I think I know Her well, I find She's changed again.
> —Cheryl Martel Hardin

WHAT MAKES A COOKBOOK WICCAN?

Although Wicca is considered one of the fastest growing religions in the United States, it is still widely misunderstood. In an effort to learn more but armed only with limited, media-driven knowledge, people have asked me, "Do the recipes contain ingredients like Eye of Newt or Wing of Bat?" and "Are there spells to make my husband do the laundry and take out the trash?" and "If I practice witchcraft, will I become rich and find love?" and finally, "Will this book teach me how to cook witches?"

And the confusion did not only rest with readers. Coauthor and Medieval historian Tara Seefeldt recognized a Medieval woodcut in the early promotional material for *The Wicca Cookbook* with a haggard old woman holding a baby next to a cauldron of boiling water that had been used to persecute women in the Middle Ages. Thereafter Tara carefully inspected each illustration to be certain it did not contain derisive images that would perpetuate negative stereotypes.

Over the last decade, we discovered that our cookbook, with its historical foundation, was a benign way for curious readers to explore witches and magic. Many readers were exposed, perhaps for the first time, to the positive aspects of a lifestyle grounded in ancient folk wisdom and came to know Wiccans as tree-hugging earth worshippers who strive to create harmony in all relationships.

Faced with the typically negative stereotypes around witches and magic, we've tried to reeducate our audience with a new understanding of Wicca as an earth-based, not spell-casting based, religion. We also tried to use humor and offered cavalier responses when asked whether or not witches still flew around on brooms. "Brooms? Oh that's so passé, nowadays we use vacuum cleaners—Dustbusters for short trips."

Persistent negative stereotypes are perfectly understandable when seen in the context of the pervasive and dangerous idea that Wiccans consort with the devil. This falsehood evolved from an ancient Eurocentric image of the male side of deity. The male god was known by many names including the Green Man, the Horned One, and Pan and symbolized the spirit of wild, verdant nature. He was believed to be as green as the woods with the legs and horns of a goat to represent his virility. When early Christians decide to eradicate the belief system of the pagans (country dwellers), or heathens (those of the heath), they demonized what was most sacred by coloring the Green Man scarlet and calling him the devil. Interestingly, modern Wiccans don't even acknowledge an evil force that would correspond to the Christian devil.

What makes a cookbook Wiccan has nothing to do with the sensationalism or typecasting that Wicca practitioners have had to endure for generations, but rather rests solely on seasonal living and intention-based action. Wicca is a way of life with traditions that originate from nature's transitions. Simply adapting your daily routine to the seasons begins to create harmony between rest and action, just as nature's cyclical cadence balances times of quiet and rejuvenation during the fall and winter with times of growth and action during the spring and summer.

The seasons themselves determined how the recipes were organized in this book. Recipes for fall include grains and the hearty root vegetables associated with the celebration of the harvest, the Autumnal Equinox, and Samhain. As nature begins winding down with shorter, cooler days and longer chillier nights, autumn rituals help us release unhelpful patterns of thought and behavior and guide us toward the depths of our souls. Winter recipes, organized around the celebrations of Yule and Imbolc, use ingredients that are naturally warming to the body and soul, such as barley, ginger, and cinnamon. Winter rituals, many of which evolved from Medieval Eurocentric traditions, remind us of the importance of family and community. Spring recipes, organized around Ostara and Beltane, abound with edible flowers and seeds, mirroring the resurgence of our domestic gardens as well as the meadows and forests—

nature's wild gardens. Not surprisingly, spring rituals represent an intuitive longing for rebirth, awakening, and cleansing. Finally, summer recipes, celebrating Litha and Lammas, include tree-and-vine-ripened fruits and vegetables symbolizing the abundance of our gardens at their peak. Summer's rituals acknowledge and honor our accomplishments and celebrate the results of our labor.

The eight Wiccan holidays are divided into four major sabbats and four minor sabbats, each one honoring and commemorating a natural, seasonal event. The major sabbats are Samhain, Imbolc, Beltane, and Lammas (also known as Lughnasad). The planting season is celebrated on Imbolc and Beltane. The harvest is observed on Samhain and Lammas. The minor sabbats of Yule (Winter Solstice), Ostara (Spring Equinox), Litha (Summer Solstice) and Mabon (Autumnal Equinox) mark the earth's relationship to the sun. Community feasting on the eight sabbats is a hallmark Wiccan celebrations and the recipes have been arranged with roughly an equal number of main dishes, side dishes, breads, drinks, and desserts for each holiday.

Wiccans choose to eat seasonal meals because we believe the food is inherently more nutritious because it has more life pulsing through it. The less time is takes for food to get from the garden to your table, the more life force from the sun and soil will be active within it. Life feeds life. To go a step further, we suggest trying an earth friendly diet that includes organic, locally grown, and even home-grown produce and proteins. Organic farming practices do not tax the environment with chemical fertilizers and toxic pesticides, while locally grown food cuts down on transportation and packaging, which saves the earth's precious resources.

Typically nonorganic vegetables, such as tomatoes, are picked when still hard and green and are chemically treated to "ripen" them yet "preserve" them so they appear pristine in the grocery store. Fascinating research has shown that locally grown food evolves to overcome the "tension" of the local environment and by ingesting foods raised in your area, you also ingest those adaptogens, with their stress-reducing properties. It is said that one can avoid being stung by bees by eating locally made honey.

Growing your own food can begin with a modest herb garden such as basil or chives. You don't need much space to grow herbs—a sunny windowsill or patio will do if you don't have a yard—but you'll add loads of flavor and gain a deeper connection to the synergetic relationship between you and the natural world.

Recipes in this cookbook contain whole, unprocessed ingredients, including, in most cases, the sauces. If we were to eliminate all processed foods from our diets, we could cut our food-related carbon footprint by almost one-third. Purchasing unprocessed foods reduces resource-wasteful packaging, which accounts for 20 percent of all the fuel consumption. And, as American portions get bigger—and Americans themselves grow larger—it wouldn't hurt any of us to eat a little less, which would automatically reduce the strain on Mother Earth herself.

It's no surprise that an earth-friendly diet is compatible with an earth-centered religion, but even tree-hugging Wiccans need a nudge toward eco-friendly habits from time to time. In fact, we all need to be looking at how we can reduce our impact on the earth and all our fellow inhabitants. We have found that most readers attracted to this book have a strong sense of connection to the earth and her creatures. Scientists call this biophilia (bio meaning life, philia meaning friendship), interpreted together the term means a reverance for life. An innate recognition and respect for all of living things is at the heart this book.

By presenting a seasonal cookbook infused with history and ceremony, we hope to offer our readers new ways to connect more deeply with nature. Even if you aren't drawn to practice of Wiccan lifestyle—or aren't even much of a cook—you will learn more about seasonal living, and you will discover time-honored lore that gives meaning to our modern traditions.

The other focus of the book—which gives it special relevance to the tenets of Wicca—is its focus on intention. Intention is a catalyst to any kind of alchemy—whether for magical or culinary pursuits. This book rests on the premise that your attitude, whether positive or negative, will affect the outcome of the dishes you prepare. In other words, how you feel is a fundamental ingredient in everything you cook. Therefore whenever you are cooking or gathering ingredients for a meal, check in with your emotional state of being and align yourself with positive, life-enriching feelings—even if it's only for a moment.

There is an old story about a grandmother who made the most delicious food for her friends and family. Everyone raved about every dish and how good they felt after a meal at her home. As she prepared her recipes, she always took a little pinch from a special jar on the counter near the stove. Breakfast, lunch, or dinner—whatever was in the jar was essential to every dish she made. What could this ingredient be? Was it cinnamon? Salt? No matter how they badgered her, she would not reveal her secret. Many years passed and many delectable meals later, the grandmother died. One day, her husband of fifty years shuffled across the kitchen and very tenderly opened his wife's special jar. He was amazed to find that it was empty, save for a small, folded slip of paper Scrawled across the paper in the familiar writing was the single and most important word: Love.

So remember to always include love in your food preparations and you are certain to create the most delicious, magical dishes.

CANDLEMAS

Candlemas (also known as Imbolc, Oimelc, Lady Day, and Brigid) is celebrated on February 2.

Candlemas is the Fire Festival dedicated to Brigid, the goddess of fire, inspiration, and sacred wells. She also represents the triple aspects of poetry, smithcraft, and healing. This is the time of year when from the darkness of winter, the seeds of light and inspiration begin to take root and grow. In an attempt to encourage the slowly waxing sunlight, you can light a candle (especially orange candles, as this color represents Divine creativity) anointed with musk, cinnamon, or rosemary oil in every room. Alternatively, you can turn on lamps with the intent to honor the sun's rebirth.

As the snowflake is the recognized symbol of this sabbat, you can recreate it with a white flower, crystal cluster, or a "captured" snowflake (a bit of snow) in a crystal container. Other traditions that you can do to celebrate this sabbat include sweeping out the old; making grain dollies, candle wheels, or sun wheels; collecting stones for magical purposes; and sharing creative work. Candle or sun wheels, symbols of the Wheel of the Year, are wreaths inlaid with eight candles—one for each sabbat. Often a young woman representing the Virgin Goddess or Candlemas Bride will enter the ceremonial site wearing the sun wheel as a means of enticing the youthful sun to return. Now is the time to visualize life flourishing with abundance, creativity, and renewed strength.

Herbs and flowers associated with Candlemas include angelica, basil, bay, benzoin, celandine, heather, myrrh, snowdrop, rowan, and all yellow flowers.

Traditional foods of Candlemas include those that represent growth, such as seeds (sesame, sunflower, pumpkin, etc.), as well as dairy foods, bread, cake, curry, peppers, onions, leeks, garlic, honey, and herbal teas.

CANDLEMAS PÂTÉ

Serves 4 to 6

1 CUP HAZELNUTS, SKINNED

1/3 CUP SESAME SEEDS

1 (8-OUNCE) PACKAGE
CREAM CHEESE

2 CLOVES GARLIC, CRUSHED

SALT AND PEPPER

2 TABLESPOONS MINCED
FRESH SAGE

2 TABLESPOONS OLIVE OIL

1/4 CUP MILK

The sesame seeds and hazelnuts in this vegetarian plate are symbolic of the new life waiting to sprout during Candlemas. Imagine those desires you want to take root and develop in the coming months. These desires may be a release from an old pain, a fresh outlook on life, a dream realized, or a new adventure. Create in your mind the situations that will enable you to manifest all that you desire. See the people who will be guiding and assisting you in reaching your goals. Visualize yourself dressing, acting, and being the authentic you, the person you long to be.

Direct your creative energy into this dish. Know that you are a perfect channel through which the Goddess can send Her inspiration. We all have the capabilities to invoke Divine inspiration.

Preheat the oven to 350°F. Place the hazelnuts and sesame seeds on separate baking sheets. Lightly roast in the oven for 7 minutes. When the nuts are cool, rub off the skins. Grind the nuts and seeds together until they resemble fine crumbs; you can use a mortar and pestle or a small hand nut grinder. If you prefer a coarse pâté, grind half the nuts and seeds finely and half coarsely.

In a small bowl, beat the cream cheese, garlic, salt and pepper to taste, sage, and oil. Add the milk. The mixture needs to be moist, as the nuts will absorb some of the liquid.

Serve chilled in ramekins or on small individual salad plates.

BRIGID'S SEEDED HUMMUS

1¹/₂ cups

2 TABLESPOONS SESAME SEEDS

3 CLOVES GARLIC, MINCED

3 TABLESPOONS FRESHLY
SQUEEZED LEMON JUICE

2 TABLESPOONS OLIVE OIL

2 TABLESPOONS PLAIN
NONFAT YOGURT

¹/₂ TEASPOON GROUND CUMIN

¹/₄ TEASPOON GROUND
CAYENNE PEPPER

1 (15-OUNCE) CAN GARBANZO
BEANS, RINSED AND DRAINED

DASH OF SALT

It is not enough that you read a spiritual book and nod in agreement. If you want to know the Goddess, you must search for Her yourself. The only truth that will ever make sense to you is that knowledge that you have tested for yourself and interpreted from your own frame of reference. Symbols and rituals will take on new meanings when you color them with your experiences and background. Who you are makes up what you see. Our individuality is akin to the limitless number of rays that emanate from the sun and the moon. No two people will ever explain the same ritual, sunset, symbol, or definition of the Goddess in exactly the same way.

The seeds of inspiration are the stepping stones toward the larger aspiration of life, just like the sesame seeds of this recipe are the beginning of the process. These steps are integral to making the end result the best it can possibly be. Trusting in the Divine inspiration that is in you will lead you toward bigger and better dreams than you ever could have hoped for. Come to understand the truth that resides within you, and the truth will set you free.

In a 6- to 8-inch skillet over medium heat, stir the sesame seeds until golden, about 5 minutes.

In a blender or food processor, combine the sesame seeds, garlic, lemon juice, olive oil, yogurt, cumin, ground cayenne pepper, and garbanzo beans. Whirl until smooth, scraping the sides often. Season with salt.

Transfer to a bowl that saves food well. Hummus may be stored in the refrigerator up to 1 month.

Hummus can be eaten on crackers, as a dip for chips, vegetables, or bread chunks, as a salad dressing, or in place of meat on a sandwich or on pita bread.

Cupid's Cold Slaw

Serves 4

Dressing

2 TABLESPOONS GRANULATED SUGAR

2 TABLESPOONS FRESHLY SQUEEZED LIME JUICE

1 TABLESPOON FISH SAUCE

1 TEASPOON SESAME OIL

1/2 TEASPOON FRESH GRATED GINGER

1/4 TEASPOON RED OR BLACK PEPPER

Slaw

4 CUPS CHINESE CABBAGE, SLICED

1/2 CUP SNOW PEAS, TRIMMED AND CUT LENGTHWISE INTO THIN STRIPS

1/2 CUP FRESH BEAN SPROUTS

1/2 CUP JICAMA, PEELED AND JULIENNED

2 TABLESPOONS GREEN ONIONS, THINLY SLICED

2 TABLESPOONS FRESH CILANTRO, FINELY CHOPPED

Cupid was the son of the Roman Venus (goddess of love) and Mercury (messenger god). In the Greek pantheon, he is known as Eros and his story is almost identical in both cultures. Venus became jealous of a human princess named Psyche (meaning "soul") who was so beloved by her subjects that they forgot to worship Venus. The goddess ordered her son to make Psyche fall in love with the vilest creature in the world, but when Cupid saw Psyche, he was so overcome by her beauty that he fell in love with her himself.

Thus began his nightly visits to Psyche's bedchamber where he whispered to her as she slept, telling her he was her mysterious husband, but begging her to never to try to see him. Psyche's older sisters grew jealous and convinced her to look at mystery lover's face by lamplight. She fell in love with Cupid instantly, but the spell was broken and Psyche found herself cast out on a barren rock. She spent endless days and nights looking for her lost lover, until at last Jupiter, king of the gods, granted Psyche the gift of immortality and she become a goddess. When Cupid, the messenger of love, and Psyche, the embodiment of soul, finally came together, they had a daughter, Voluptas, also called Hedone, which means pleasure and from which the word *hedonism* is derived.

To make the dressing, in a small bowl, whisk together the sugar, lime juice, fish sauce, sesame oil, ginger, and pepper. In a large bowl, combine the cabbage and remaining ingredients. Add the dressing and toss well to coat. Chill for 30 minutes.

Note: *Vegetarian fish sauce is an acceptable substitute.*

Walnut-Onion Bread

The walnuts in this bread are a consecrated symbol within the Candlemas celebration because they represent all that is yet to manifest. A spell is the seed of the future manifestation, just like the walnut is the seed of the future tree.

Magic is affected by sources outside of ourselves at moments. Spell casting can be so exciting, and yet frustrating, because the result can be altered based on our individuality, the arrangement of the cosmos, and the highest need of all life at that particular moment in time.

We can achieve our desired conclusion in our incantations, albeit not always in a form we recognize. The movement of one planet in particular can essentially reverse the effect of a spell.

Spell casting is an oral communication spoken aloud to the Universe. Mercury rules communication. About four times a year, Mercury appears to be moving backward, which is known as a Mercury retrograde. Each retrograde lasts three to four weeks. When we experience a Mercury retrograde, all forms of communication are altered, such as mail service, telephones, relationships, computers, electronics, and, of course, spell casting.

During this interlude, our systems are scattered, and chaos seems to be at its peak. But in this confusion, a great lesson is offered. When everything has been rearranged, a fresh way of looking at a problem presents itself, a trait we forgot or did not know we possessed comes to light, and we rise to the occasion. But we must let go of all expectations and be prepared to laugh at the unpredictability of a Mercury retrograde—or find ourselves quite frustrated. We can experience success as long as we are willing to accept the lessons and laugh, laugh, laugh.

Jennifer DeVeoux, who firmly believes in food's innate healing powers—especially when charged with positive intent—gives this recipe to us.

Continues on next page

2 loaves, serving 8

1 (1/4-OUNCE) PACKAGE ACTIVE
DRY YEAST

1 CUP WARM MILK

4 TABLESPOONS BUTTER, AT ROOM
TEMPERATURE

2/3 CUP BREAD FLOUR

1 1/2 TEASPOONS GRANULATED
SUGAR

1 1/2 TEASPOONS SALT

1/2 CUP FINELY DICED RED
OR PURPLE ONION

3/4 CUP CHOPPED WALNUTS

Blend the yeast and 1/4 cup of the warm milk. Let stand for 5 to 10 minutes, until foaming.

Add the butter to the remaining 3/4 cup of milk; let the butter melt. In a large bowl, mix the flour with the sugar and salt. Make a well in the center of the flour, and pour in the milk and butter mixture. Mix until well blended. Let cool for 5 minutes. Add the yeast mixture and mix again until well blended.

Turn the dough out onto a floured board. Knead until elastic and soft, approximately 10 to 15 minutes. Place the kneaded dough in a greased bowl and cover tightly with plastic wrap. Let rise for 2 hours in a warm, draft-free place, or until doubled.

Punch down the dough. Turn the dough out onto a floured board. Knead in the onion and walnuts until evenly distributed. Cut into two pieces and shape into long, thin loaves, about 1 1/2 inches thick. Let stand for 45 minutes, uncovered, in a warm, draft-free place. Preheat the oven to 400°F. Transfer the loaves to a parchment paper- or waxed paper-lined baking sheet.

Bake for 25 to 30 minutes, until the bread is golden brown and sounds hollow when you tap it.

This bread accompanies well most soft cheeses, such as goat, Brie, or even cream cheese.

Note: Whenever you combine yeast with a liquid, be it milk or water, make sure that the liquid is warm. Either measure the temperature with a thermometer (between 105°F and 125°F or go by touch (the water should be warm to the touch, but not hot; the temperature of a warm bath is perfect). With all yeast breads, you must first test the yeast. To test, dissolve the yeast in 1/2 cup of warm water or milk with a pinch of sugar. The liquid should bubble, proving the yeast is active. Then follow the instructions.

Brigid's Magical Bread

1 loaf, serving 6

---

1 (1/4-OUNCE) PACKAGE ACTIVE
DRY YEAST

1 1/4 CUP PLUS TWO
TABLESPOONS WATER

1/3 CUP HONEY

2 CUPS WHOLE-WHEAT FLOUR

1/3 CUP CHOPPED RED ROSE PETALS

2 TABLESPOONS POPPY SEEDS

1/3 CUP VEGETABLE OIL (OPTIONAL)

The only desire Brigid had was to be a bride. In the Middle Ages, children carried kirn or grain dollies, symbolizing Brigid, around the village in search of her husband. Even today many pagans dress a dolly as the bride and lay her in either a small corncrib or wooden bed. They may even throw in male fertility symbols, such as nuts or seeds into her bed.

If you are trying to win someone's love, you may be able to entice him or her with this bread. If you are trying to attract a blond individual, add 1 teaspoon of vanilla extract. If it's the affections of a dark person whose love you are seeking, add 1/4 cup finely ground walnuts to the mixture. If a red-haired person has caught your interest, add 1/4 cup of finely ground almonds. Lastly, if you love a stubborn individual who is slow to move into your embrace, add 1 teaspoon of lemon extract to open his or her mind to your amorous affections.

Judith "Jade" Defrain, Wiccan High Priestess and owner of Eye of the Cat, located in Long Beach, California, a witch's-everything store, donated this multigenerational recipe.

Preheat the oven to 375°F. Blend the yeast, water, and honey. Let stand for 5 to 10 minutes, until foaming. Mix in the flour, rose petals, poppy seeds, and oil or other additional ingredients, and knead. Add additional flour if the dough sticks to the side of the bowl.

Mold the dough into a ball. Cover with a cloth for 1 hour. Punch down the dough in the center and knead for approximately 5 minutes.

Place the dough in a greased loaf pan for about 1 hour, until doubled. Bake for 35 to 40 minutes.

Puffy Omelet

Serves 2 to 4

2 TO 4 LARGE EGGS, SEPARATED

1 TABLESPOON MILK PER EGG

1/2 TABLESPOON BUTTER PER EGG

SALT AND PEPPER

3/4 CUP GRATED
GORGONZOLA CHEESE

4 TO 6 SPRIGS OF ROSEMARY OR
SLICES OF YOUR FAVORITE FRUIT,
FOR GARNISH

The Candlemas celebration rejoices in the opportunities that await us as we venture from our cozy homes to admire a world waking from a long winter's nap. The sun is returning with great force now. The days are continuing to lengthen, and the darkness of winter is receding.

This ceaseless rebirth of the sun is a comforting part of the turn of the Wheel of Life. With the sun's birthday, our limitless Universe offers renewed strength and vitality.

The rosemary in this recipe gives us the opportunity to bless and thank our homes for protecting and shielding us from the harsh coldness of the winter months. Since this holiday is also known as the Fire Festival, try anointing a lightbulb with rosemary oil or burning dried rosemary sprigs in a show of your gratitude. You can also light an orange candle, which resembles the returning sun and symbolizes spirituality.

Preheat the oven to 350°F. In a bowl, beat the egg whites until they stand in soft peaks. In another bowl, beat the egg yolks until slightly thickened and paler yellow. Add the milk to the yolk mixture. Season with salt and pepper.

Melt 1/2 tablespoon of butter per egg in a large, heavy, ovenproof skillet until sizzling. Fold the yolk mixture into the beaten egg whites. Pour the mixture into the skillet. Decrease heat to low. Cook slowly until the egg mixture is light brown underneath, about 10 minutes. There will still be a bit of bubbling, and the mixture will look moist.

Place the skillet in the oven and bake until the mixture is light brown on top and no imprint shows when the mixture is lightly touched with a finger, about 10 to 15 minutes.

Remove from the oven and make a 1/2-inch-deep crease across the middle of the omelet with a spatula. Sprinkle 1/2 cup of the cheese onto the omelet. Slip the spatula underneath, tip the skillet to loosen the omelet, and fold in half without breaking it. Roll the omelet top-side down onto a hot platter (metal or ceramic works best).

Top with the remaining cheese, and garnish with sprigs of rosemary and/ or fruit slices. Serve at once.

FRUMENTY

Serves 4

3 CUPS CHICKEN, VEGETABLE,
OR BEEF BROTH

1 CUP BULGUR WHEAT

PINCH OF SAFFRON

1 LARGE EGG

Frumenty was and is traditionally accompanied by venison. During the Middle Ages, it was the standard dish eaten by great lords and senior clerics. In this dish, we offer a pinch of saffron. The nobility loved their saffron! This yellow flower represented much to someone of high standing and "good" blood. Saffron has customarily been the most expensive seasoning due to the labor required for harvesting the individual stamens.

When using saffron, try to obtain saffron that is less than one year old, has a strong aroma, and is brilliant orange in color. The herb has a bitter flavor that is characteristically warm, which lends itself well to this porridge/side dish.

Frumenty is often consumed during the winter. Because of the use of a flower, it is a symbolic dish, a sign that spring will return. It makes a good side dish to eat with strongly flavored meat and game dishes, but plain frumenty is best today as a breakfast porridge.

Bring the broth to a boil in a saucepan. Stir in the bulgur wheat and saffron. Cover and simmer over low heat for 35 to 45 minutes. Beat the egg and add it to the mixture. Continue to simmer, stirring occasionally, for 3 minutes.

Variation
For richer porridge, substitute 1¹/₂ cups of milk for 1¹/₂ cups of broth and 2 egg yolks instead of 1 egg.

CRUSTADE OF CHICKEN

Serves 6

1/2 (17 1/4-OUNCE) PACKAGE
PUFF PASTRY

3 CUPS CHICKEN BROTH

4 BONELESS, SKINLESS
CHICKEN BREASTS

2/3 CUP WHITE WINE

1/2 TEASPOON PEPPER

4 CLOVES GARLIC, MINCED

1/4 CUP CHOPPED MUSHROOMS

2 TABLESPOONS CRUMBLED
CRISP BACON

2 TABLESPOONS DRIED
CRANBERRIES OR DRY-PACKED
SUNDRIED TOMATOES

3 LARGE EGGS

SALT AND PEPPER

1/2 TEASPOON GROUND GINGER

Due to its affordability, chicken was frequently enjoyed by the peasantry in the Middle Ages. Over the years, people have become quite creative in the ways they prepare poultry. Candlemas celebrates and honors that creative nature, with its focus on the creative outlet of poetry, healing, smithcraft, and cooking.

The ways in which we perform the everyday miracle of our lives is poetry in and of itself. Every day we paint on the canvas of our lives and either bring healing or pain. Every day we mold our expectations of the future, assemble what we value in the present, and shape the way we view the past. One way in which you can become more mindful of the life you want to create is by asking the Goddess for conscious awareness and recognition of the lesson and guidance that are being offered. Begin by grounding yourself. One way to do this is to slow your breathing. Take ten deep breaths. Light a purple candle for wisdom. Say

I now am aware of the messages that are being sent to me.
I am open to all the good the Universe offers abundantly.
I welcome my blessings, both hidden and those easy to see.
I am willing to follow Divine guidance given just for me.

Preheat the oven to 350°F. Roll out the sheet of pastry and line an 8-inch soufflé dish. Crimp the top edges of the crust.

In a large, heavy pot, combine the broth, chicken, wine, pepper, and garlic. Cook very slowly over medium-low heat for 1 1/2 hours, until the chicken is very tender.

In a small skillet, sauté the mushrooms lightly in butter.

Drain the broth from the chicken and save the broth. Cut the chicken into very small pieces and mix it with the mushrooms. Add the bacon and cranberries and mix. Spread this mixture over the crust in the soufflé dish. Beat the eggs. Season with salt, pepper, and ginger. Add 1 cup of the broth to the egg mixture. Pour over the meat in the soufflé dish. Bake for 25 minutes.

Blood Orange Mahi Mahi

Serves 2

1 BLOOD ORANGE

1/2 CUP AVOCADO, CUBED

1/3 CUP CHOPPED RED ONION

1 TEASPOON CILANTRO, CHOPPED

2 TEASPOONS RED JALAPEÑO, MINCED

2 TEASPOONS FRESHLY SQUEEZED LIME JUICE

SALT AND FRESHLY GROUND PEPPER

2 TEASPOONS OLIVE OIL

2 (6-OUNCE) FRESH MAHI MAHI FILLETS

2 TABLESPOONS COTIJA CHEESE, CRUMBLED

The blood orange is a type of sweet orange that has a red blush to its skin and a scarlet, crimson, or purple flesh. Blood oranges are sometimes called the connoisseur's or gourmet's citrus because they have a sweet-tart flavor with rich overtones of raspberries and strawberries. You will find blood oranges at farmers' markets from early winter through spring.

The blood-red color of these oranges makes them perfect using at Candlemas or Imbolc as red and white are typically associated with these winter celebrations. White symbolizes the snow and red is represents the hearth fire or Brigid's eternal flame.

Peel the orange, separate the fruit into segments and place in a bowl. Add the avocado, onion, jalapeño, cilantro, and lime juice. Season with salt and stir gently. Heat the oil in skillet over medium-high heat. Sprinkle the fish with salt and pepper. Add the fish to the skillet and sauté until brown and cooked through, about 5 minutes per side. Plate the mahi mahi, spoon the salsa over the fish, sprinkle with the cheese, and serve.

Imbolc Moon Cookies

About 5 dozen cookies

Icing

**2 CUPS SIFTED
CONFECTIONERS' SUGAR**

1 TEASPOON VANILLA EXTRACT

2 1/2 TABLESPOONS WATER

1 CUP BUTTER, SOFTENED

1 1/4 CUPS GRANULATED SUGAR

**1 TEASPOON VANILLA OR
PEPPERMINT EXTRACT**

2 TEASPOONS GRATED LEMON PEEL

1/4 TEASPOON SALT

1 1/3 CUPS ALL-PURPOSE FLOUR

1 1/2 CUPS GROUND WALNUTS

These cookies received their name for their similarity in appearance to the full moon. The moon's silvery essence resembles clear crystals found deep within Mother Nature's caverns. All crystals and precious gems possess healing properties. But over time they can get worn down, and their healing powers become as murky as the crystals appear to be. The night of the full moon is the best time to charge crystals with renewed strength. To do this, rinse your crystals with seawater or saltwater. Set all the crystals and gems on a special cloth in the moonlight as you enjoy these luminescent treats. Say

> Now I invoke thee, O Mother of mine.
> To renew with strength, these crystals of thine.
> Help me to reflect your pure Divine light,
> Choosing a life that is healing and bright.

To make the icing, combine the confectioners' sugar, vanilla, and water, mixing until well blended. Thin the icing with additional drops of water if glaze is too thick.

Preheat the oven to 375°F. In a large bowl, cream the butter, sugar, and vanilla extract until fluffy and light. Mix the lemon peel, salt, flour, and walnuts in a bowl. In increments, add the flour mixture to the butter and sugar. Mix until well blended. Cover and chill thoroughly for at least 2 hours.

When the dough is chilled, roll it to a thickness of 1/8 inch, and cut with a crescent moon cookie cutter.

Place the cookies 1/2 inch apart on an ungreased baking sheet. Bake for 8 to 10 minutes.

After baking, allow the cookies to stand for 5 minutes. Spread the icing over tops of cookies while they are still warm.

Note: If you can't find a crescent moon-shaped cookie cutter, you can use a circular cutter and cut a curved line in the middle, then roll the excess dough from the cut-out cookie, and repeat.

SNOWFLAKE CAKES

These light and powdery cookies resemble the snowflake that is the symbol of the Candlemas holiday. Imagine snow as symbolic of the Divine Source and its unlimited benevolence, reflecting that pureness. We, too, are molded after a Divine goodness. But we have free will, and some humans choose to alter their innate goodness and become something they were never intended to be.

The following spell offers protection as well as suggests an alternative path toward kindness that your fellow humans can follow. Begin taking three deep breaths through the mouth and feel the strength of the Goddess filling your body. Imagine an illuminating white light encasing you like a dome that nothing evil or bad can penetrate.

Light three candles: a white candle to represent your pure intent, a pink candle to symbolize unconditional love, and a red candle to portray action. Imagine your adversary as a lost soul, one who has ventured from the path of goodness to the blackness of a personal hell. You don't need to pity this person, but just see him or her as a confused spiritual being. This reminds us that they have no solid ground, no sturdy foundation on which to make their false and accusatory statements and deeds. Now visualize the person coming toward you. Say firmly

You no longer have the power to harm me.
I will myself free of you.
My being mirrors that of the Divine Source.
Go with the Mother.

Imagine this person bouncing off your protective shield. See rays of your white light spinning off your dome and encircling your enemy. Your enemy may choose to see this entanglement as confining, or in time he or she may come to recognize the white light as loving, embracing arms. However, this light is interpreted is of no consequence to you; either way, your work is done. Allow the candles to continue to burn. Visualize your surrounding

Continues on next page

SNOWFLAKE CAKES, continued

4 dozen cookies

3/4 CUP CHOPPED PECANS

2 CUPS BUTTER, SOFTENED

1/2 CUP PLUS 1/3 CUP
CONFECTIONERS' SUGAR

2 TEASPOONS VANILLA EXTRACT

2 1/4 CUPS ALL-PURPOSE FLOUR

white light growing in strength and radiance. Whatever rays spin off your dome have no effect on you, for as you continue to build power, you emanate more light. You are now protected by the light and love that is your Divine right.

Your enemy's malicious intent no longer will have an effect on you but will boomerang off your protective shield and reflect back on themselves, whereupon they have the choice to accept or reject this negative energy. Alternatively you can visualize the negative energy plummeting to the earth where the Mother can transform the energy to a positive state. To manifest a positive result from this spell, and all spells you cast, your intention must be pure and for the good of all. Others may wish to send out negative energy, but in doing so, they hex themselves three times. Each time we do good, it is always returned unto us threefold. Remember, the most sacred place is where an ancient hatred once reigned supreme.

Preheat the oven to 350°F. Place the pecans in a baking pan and toast for 5 to 8 minutes. Once toasted, set aside until completely cooled. Place the cooled pecans in a blender or food processor and grind until very finely chopped, but not powdery and oily (you can also use a hand nut grinder). In a large bowl, cream the butter, the 1/2 cup of confectioners' sugar, and vanilla until fluffy and well blended. Gradually add the pecans to the butter mixture. Sift the flour into the butter mixture and stir until the dough holds together.

Pull off pieces of dough and roll between your hands into generous 1-inch balls. Place the balls about 1 1/4 inches apart on two greased baking sheets. Increase the oven temperature to 400°F. Bake 1 sheet at a time, until the cookies are faintly tinged with brown, about 10 to 12 minutes. Rotate the sheet halfway through baking for even browning. Remove the sheet to a wire rack and let it stand until the cakes firm.

Roll the warm cakes in the remaining confectioners' sugar. Let them cool more on the wire rack. Roll them in the sugar again.

Note: To save, place the cookies in an airtight container, and if stacked, place waxed paper in between layers of cakes. Cookies will remain fresh for up to one week.

Valentine's Chocolate

Serves 4 to 6

4 1/2 CUPS MILK

4 OUNCES SEMISWEET CHOCOLATE

5 TABLESPOONS
GRANULATED SUGAR

1/2 TEASPOON GROUND CINNAMON

1/2 TEASPOON VANILLA EXTRACT

1/8 TEASPOON ALLSPICE

1 OUNCE PEPPERMINT SCHNAPPS
OR WHISKEY

4 TO 6 STICKS CINNAMON,
FOR GARNISH

Chocolate did not really become known in Europe until Europeans went to the Americas. In the seventeenth century, the first account of a drink made from the cocoa bean was discussed. But it wasn't until the eighteenth and nineteenth centuries that a chocolate drink became well known and widespread in Europe. Later, after the drink was incorporated into their diet, people began experimenting with chocolate as a dessert. Because Valentine's Day falls within the Candlemas season, we have incorporated the love associated with this day as part of the warmth and energy of this time of year. A Valentine's ritual for Candlemas is to weave a lover's knot. The lover's knot was made by young men for their sweethearts as a love token or courting favor. Many of the designs that were used were often highly individual and sometimes passed down through families from generation to generation. This symbol of two intersecting circles side by side can either be woven into clothing or fashioned with a ribbon or yarn and tied to a garment. Love and merriment are essential in our lives. The joy of giving and receiving special treats such as chocolate is sacred, as well as just plain fun. Chocolate is now one of the most common treats given during the Candlemas holiday for Wiccans as well as others. After a Candlemas circle, we often offer this drink to our guests in honor of the love we share together.

In a large saucepan, combine the milk, chocolate, sugar, cinnamon, vanilla, allspice, and alcohol. Bring to a boil, stirring constantly. Beat the mixture until it stops boiling and become slightly frothy.

Serve in mugs and garnish with cinnamon sticks.

Note: This drink can be made without alcohol. Use 1 teaspoon of peppermint flavoring instead of schnapps or whiskey.

DIVINELY SPICED WINE

Serves 10 to 12

4 CUPS RED GRAPE JUICE

6 CUPS RED WINE

2 TO 3 STICKS CINNAMON

1/2 TABLESPOON WHOLE CLOVES

1/2 TEASPOON ALLSPICE

1 TEASPOON GROUND CARDAMOM

3/4 CUP FIRMLY PACKED LIGHT
BROWN SUGAR

 iccans use a variety of tools to help divine the correct path for their highest spiritual journey. One way to incorporate Mother Nature into your spirituality is by collecting stones, a pastime of the Candlemas celebration. Initiate your search by imagining the stones you want to find. The quest may take you to a park, the beach, the mountains, or the desert. Collect thirteen stones. We recommend looking for smooth stones no bigger than one to two inches.

Gather your stones together and place them in a circle. Light a green candle. Green is the color of nature and healing. Bless the stones with your intention, love, and light by holding them to your heart. As you enjoy the wine, polish the stones, ridding them of all dirt and debris. Visualize thirteen symbols that have special significance in your life; they might include a tree, heart, male or female figure, sun, moon, animal guide, water, or fire. With a permanent marker or burin, draw or cut each figure onto a stone. Once each is designed, glaze them. You will then have your own set of divination stones.

When you find yourself plagued with a problem, cast a small circle approximately one foot in diameter. Draw a circle in the air with your athame or forefinger. Welcome all your protective guides. Center yourself, then throw your stones into the circle. Those stones that turn upward are sent from above to help direct you. Look on the special meanings that connect you to these symbols for guidance. As you become more familiar with casting stones, their definitions will expand in significance, and you will more readily accept direction from the Universe.

In a large saucepan, combine the juice and wine. Add the spices and brown sugar. Bring to a boil. Decrease heat and simmer for 10 to 15 minutes. Adjust the sweetness according to your personal taste by adding more sugar.

SPRING EQUINOX

Spring Equinox (also known as Vernal Equinox, Festival of Trees, Alban Eilir, Ostara, and Eostar Ritual) is celebrated on the first day of spring.

This sabbat acknowledges and honors all life, now burgeoning with new growth. Altars are adorned with flowers, potted plants, candles, incense, or any sign of life. Eggs, a symbol of fertility and new life, are decorated. You can choose to decorate wooden eggs or hollow eggshells and fill them with symbols of spring, such as perfume, confetti, lavender, or sage. Hang the eggs by colorful strings or yarn on trees. The egg is said to have received its importance to this sabbat from a lowly rabbit that so wished to please the Goddess Eostre (the German goddess of spring and the dawn) that he placed gaily festooned eggs in her honor.

During the Spring Equinox, it is important to give thanks to each of the four directions for the gifts they offer. Traditionally, the east represents the beginning of all things, akin to the sun rising from the east. The directions are listed deosil (clockwise or sunwise). East symbolizes air, and it rules mental and intuitive work. South represents fire, and it rules healing and destruction. West connotes water and the womb, and it rules emotions and the subconscious mind. North signifies the earth, and it rules growth and material gains. Other ways that you can celebrate this sabbat are by collecting wildflowers, planting an herb garden, taking a meditative walk, doing needlework, or engaging in creative work with herbs.

Foods associated with the Spring Equinox include items that represent fertility, such as milk punch, hot cross buns, leafy green vegetables, foods made with flowers, and honey cakes.

White Sage House Blessing Ceremony

White sage (*Salvia alba*) has been used for centuries by Native Americans for a variety of blessing ceremonies. For this ritual, gather ten fresh sage stems and leaves into a bundle with some colorful thread, string, or yarn. The color you select will convey a specific message, so the intent of the blessing must be established first. For example, if you feel disconnected from Spirit, choose orange thread, as the color orange represents spirituality. If you feel upset or frazzled, use blue string, as blue symbolizes calmness, tranquility, and peace. If you feel tired or low on energy, red is the best choice as it represents vibrant high energy. Other colors and their meanings include pink for love; yellow for peace; green for healing or growth; purple for divine protection and knowledge; gray for fear; black for the unknown; white for truth and purity; and brown for grounding.

Once you've selected the appropriate color and tied up your bundle, hang the sage upside down and allow it to dry for two to three days. When you're ready to perform the blessing, ignite one end of the sage bundle, using a sea shell to catch the ashes. Then use a feather to direct the smoke away from you in a sweeping motion. Say or chant:

I bless this house with protective sage.
I cleanse and wash it with love and light.
I banish all negative energy,
And seal its walls with Goddess might.

Direct the smoke to every corner of every room, around every window and door, and over every drain and toilet. Also known as smudging, this ritual will clear your house of all unwanted energy and prevent negativity from entering as it seals in the positive life force. All who enter will feel the protective warmth, serenity, and love permeating throughout.

This recipe comes from Delilah Snell, owner/proprietor of the eco-friendly The Road Less Traveled Store and an all-around sassy woman who teaches classes on food preserving throughout Southern California.

WILD WOMAN WHITE SAGE JELLY

2 dozen 4-ounce jars

1½ CUPS APPLE JUICE OR
WHITE WINE

1 CUP WATER

1 CUP WHITE WINE OR
CIDER VINEGAR

1 CUP WHITE SAGE, CHOPPED

1 (1¾-OUNCE) PACKAGE
POWDERED PECTIN

5¼ CUPS GRANULATED SUGAR

24 (4-OUNCE) CANNING JARS

In a stainless steel pan, combine all the liquids, add the sage, and bring to a boil. Remove from the heat and let steep for 15 minutes. Strain the mixture, and measure 3¼ cups of the herb infusion. Transfer to a large pot and whisk in the pectin. Bring to a boil over high heat, stirring frequently. Add the sugar all at once and return to a boil. Continue boiling for 1 minute. Remove from the heat and skim the foam.

Wash the jars. Sterilize the lids in boiling water for 10 minutes to soften the adhesive agent. Pour the jelly into clean jars, filling each jar to three-quarters full. For a snug fit, wipe the rim of each jar before securing the lid.

Note: For more information on food preservation techniques, visit the National Center for Home Food Preservation website.

QUENELLES

Serves 4

2 1/2 CUPS FRESH BREAD CRUMBS

2/3 CUP MILK

1 POUND GROUND BEEF OR
TURKEY, VERY FINELY GROUND

1 CUP BUTTER, SOFTENED

2 EGG YOLKS

4 LARGE EGGS, SEPARATED

PINCH OF GRATED NUTMEG

1 TABLESPOON MINCED
FRESH PARSLEY

1 TEASPOON MINCED
FRESH THYME

SALT AND PEPPER

PEAS, BOILED AND BUTTERED,
ENOUGH TO SERVE 4

CARROTS, STEAMED OR BOILED
AND BUTTERED, ENOUGH TO
SERVE 4

2 1/2 CUPS BROWN OR
MUSHROOM GRAVY

One of the favored dishes of the Spring Equinox is quenelles. The word *quenelles* is believed to come from the Anglo-Saxon word *knyll*, which means "to pound," as the ingredients are pounded before cooking. Quenelles can be made with various kinds of meat, cheese, or potatoes. They are much like Swedish meatballs.

Herb work and lore are a big part of Wicca and are customary practices for this holiday. Either purchase dried herbs and combine them in special pouches for use as amulets, teas, and other magical purposes, or mix them with purified water to use as spritzes. You may choose to plant your own herb garden (see Growing and Using Herbs, beginning on page 23). Working in a garden is meditative spiritual work that helps connect you to the Mother. You will find yourself more grounded when you dig your fingers in Her porous soil. While your body is working, flushing out aggression, or pouring love back to Her who gives so freely, your mind is free to wander. Often, after just a few minutes in the garden, we come away with solutions to problems, a calm state of connectedness, and a sense of accomplishment.

Soak the bread crumbs in the milk, just enough to coat and make them wet. In a large bowl, pound together the meat, butter, and bread crumbs. Add the 2 egg yolks and mix well. Add the remaining egg yolks and spices. Season with salt and pepper. Pound the mixture again.

In a separate bowl, beat the egg whites until stiff. Gently fold the egg whites into the mixture. Shape into ovals with two large spoons. Place the ovals into a lightly buttered, shallow saucepan. Cover the ovals with boiling water carefully. Lay buttered aluminum foil on top. Over low heat, poach gently for 10 minutes.

Prepare the peas and the carrots, and transfer them to the serving dish you will use. Remove the quenelles from the pan with a slotted spoon and place them on the bed of peas and carrots. Serve with brown or mushroom gravy.

Note: You can substitute with 1 pound of vegetable nature burger mixed with 2 cups of water.

Stuffed Nasturtiums

Serves 4

1 (8-OUNCE) PACKAGE
CREAM CHEESE

1/2 CUP CHOPPED NUTS,
ANY VARIETY

1/4 CUP CHIVES

1 CUP SLICED WATERCRESS

16 NASTURTIUMS, LIGHTLY
WASHED

Springtime has come and with it the beautiful bobbing heads of the season's flowering beauties. Dishes made with flowers have been a preferred treat of the vernal season since the Middle Ages. Nasturtiums, in particular, are favored.

Nasturtiums originated in Peru. From there, this low-maintenance flower seduced gardeners and nature lovers throughout Western Europe. The word nasturtium translates into "nose twister." This distinction most likely came from the flower's perky, peppery smell.

Nasturtiums vary in color from bright orange to sunshine yellow. They are one of the most popular edible flowers and are used in a variety of dishes. Nasturtiums also have a slight tangy taste that makes a good combination with the watercress in this appetizer.

Combine the cream cheese, nuts, chives, and watercress, mixing well. Grasp a nasturtium. With a teaspoon, gently spoon some of the mixture into the flower. Repeat for each nasturtium.

Springtime Quiche

Serves 8

1 (9-INCH) PIECRUST
(RECIPE FOLLOWS)

1½ CUPS GRATED CHEDDAR
CHEESE

⅛ CUP DICED MUSHROOMS

⅛ CUP CHOPPED TOMATOES

¼ CUP CHOPPED HAM

3 LARGE EGGS, BEATEN

1½ CUPS HALF-AND-HALF

Piecrust

1¼ CUPS ALL-PURPOSE FLOUR

1 TEASPOON OF SALT

½ CUP BUTTER, CHILLED

2½ TABLESPOONS COLD WATER

 ggs were, and still are, especially enjoyed during the Spring Equinox. They represent reproduction, fertility, abundance, birth, renewal, and resurrection.

Many crafts involve eggs. One of our favorites is decorating hollowed-out eggshells. With a bamboo skewer, poke two holes in an egg—a bigger one in the bottom and a smaller one at top. Blow out the contents through the bottom. Let the eggshell dry for 30 minutes. With a pencil, draw your design, then go over it with a thin black marker. Fill in with watercolors or crayons.

Another way to decorate eggs is steeped in symbolic meaning from the Slavic countries. The dye colors come from nature: yellow onion skins for yellow, beets for pink, blueberries for light blue, blackberries for lavender, spinach and kale for green, or carrots for orange. Mince 1 cup of each vegetable. Boil separately for 20 minutes. Strain out the vegetables and add 2 tablespoons of vinegar per cup of dye. Draw your design with a clear wax crayon. Dip the egg in the dye until it reaches the intensity of color that you prefer. Although many designs are painted on eggs, it is customary in the Ukraine to depict an evergreen tree with deer nibbling at its roots.

Sift the flour into a mixing bowl. Add the salt and mix well with a fork or wooden spoon. Cut the butter into the flour mixture, using a pastry cutter (although two knives used in a crisscross cutting motion will also work) until the mixture resembles coarse crumbs. Stirring with a fork, add water, 1 tablespoon at a time, until the mixture forms a stiff dough.

Roll the dough into a circle. Line a pie plate with the dough, trimming the excess from the edges.

Cover the bottom of the piecrust with grated cheese. Mix together vegetables and ham and add this to the pie. Combine the beaten eggs and half-and-half and pour over the filling.

Bake at 350°F for 1 hour.

Note: For a crisper crust, substitute about 2 to 3 tablespoons of solid vegetable shortening for the same amount of butter.

Goddess Athena Pitas

Serves 4

4 LARGE WHOLE-WHEAT OR
SESAME SEED PITAS, SLICED IN HALF

1/2 CUP SHREDDED
ROMAINE LETTUCE

1/2 CUP SLICED CHESHIRE OR
OTHER HARD CHEESE

2 PLUM TOMATOES, DICED

1 ROASTED RED BELL PEPPER,
SLICED

1/2 PURPLE OR VIDALIA ONION,
THINLY SLICED

1 (4-OUNCE) CAN BLACK OLIVES,
SLICED OR DICED

1 AVOCADO, SLICED

1/2 CUP SPROUTS

1/4 CUP SESAME SEEDS, TOASTED

1/4 CUP SUNFLOWER SEEDS,
TOASTED

GREEN GODDESS DRESSING
(RECIPE FOLLOWS)

The goddess Athena is associated with the Spring Equinox because both the goddess and the holiday are associated with high intelligence and sharp mental acuity. A four-day festival is devoted to this deity, which is held from March 19 to 23. One of her gifts to the people is the olive tree, which provides shade from the blazing sun, oil for food and lamps, and delicious olives, such as the ones offered in this springtime sandwich.

Athena is known as the goddess of wisdom. Her totem animal is the owl. This magnificent bird sat atop her shoulders and revealed unseen truths to Athena, which she used to benefit humankind. The owl's powers helped the goddess expand her understanding and create inventions such as the plow and rake.

You can also call upon owl medicine to help you perceive new solutions to life's challenges. Either imagine you are the silent owl, with keen powers of observation, or envision the great bird sitting on your shoulder. Since the owl is a creature of the night, it is best to perform this meditation after the sun has set, preferably after the moon as risen. Ask the owl to befriend you and lend you some of its wisdom so that you may see clearly with a judicious heart and an insightful mind.

Lightly toast the pita halves and let cool. Stuff the pitas in this order: lettuce, cheese, tomatoes, peppers, onions, olives, avocado, and sprouts. Sprinkle the seeds on top.

Drizzle about 1 tablespoon of dressing into each pita.

Continues on next page

Green Goddess Dressing

1 CUP MAYONNAISE

1/2 CUP SOUR CREAM

**1/4 CUP MINCED FRESH CHIVES OR
SCALLIONS**

1/4 CUP MINCED FRESH PARSLEY

**1 TABLESPOON FRESHLY SQUEEZED
LEMON JUICE**

**1 TABLESPOON WHITE WINE
VINEGAR**

1 TEASPOON SOY SAUCE

1/4 TEASPOON SESAME OIL

**1/2 TEASPOON SESAME SEEDS,
TOASTED**

SALT AND PEPPER

To make the dressing, mix all the ingredients in a small bowl until well blended.

GUMBO

Serves 8 to 10

Rice

2 CUPS WHITE RICE, UNCOOKED

4 CUPS WATER

5 TO 7 TABLESPOONS OLIVE OIL

2/3 CUP ALL-PURPOSE FLOUR

1 LARGE ONION, DICED

2 RED BELL PEPPERS, DICED

6 STALKS CELERY, DICED

7 TO 8 CUPS CHICKEN BROTH

2 (15-OUNCE) CANS WHOLE
TOMATOES

3 BAY LEAVES

SALT AND PEPPER

1 TO 2 POUNDS FRESH FISH
FILLETS (FLOUNDER OR SOLE
TASTES BEST)

3/4 POUND FRESH SHRIMP, PEELED
AND DEVEINED

FILÉ POWDER

Southern cooking involves cooking from the heart. Like Wiccans, many Southerners believe that people pour their emotions into food preparation and that feelings can drastically affect the taste of a meal.

The Spring Equinox is when many of Mother Earth's creatures are born or perhaps hatched, including fish. The Spring Equinox also marks the sun leaving the sign of Pisces. People born under the Pisces sign often transcend into luminous fluidity like the mermaid and water from which they were born. The Pisces symbol represents not just fish, but also the ocean—the birthplace of all that is. With this gumbo, let's celebrate the birth of the fish, honor Mother Ocean, and bring the power of new beginning into our being.

This recipe comes from the kitchen of Bill Hurt—and the South.

To prepare the rice, mix the rice and water and a little olive oil. Cook in the oven for 2 hours, until all the water is absorbed. Cooking rice slowly reflects the Southern cooking style. If you are pressed for time, cook the rice for 20 minutes on the stove.

Make a roux by warming 3 to 4 tablespoons of the olive oil in a skillet. Add the flour and increase the temperature until it is hot enough to brown the flour. Stir continuously until the mixture turns the color of a new copper penny. Be careful not to let it burn.

In another pan, warm 2 to 3 tablespoons of olive oil. Sauté the vegetables until tender. Add the broth, tomatoes, and bay leaves. Season with salt and pepper. Bring to a boil and simmer for 20 minutes.

Preheat the oven to 325°F. Add the roux to the vegetable mixture, mixing well. Add the fish and shrimp. Simmer until cooked through, about 10 to 12 minutes. Remove bay leaves. Add filé powder until it is the desired thickness. If the mixture is not thick enough, add more flour.

Serve the gumbo with the rice.

Note: Filé powder (powdered sassafras leaves), the essential ingredient in this soup, can be bought at seafood markets or places that specialize in Southern cooking.

VIOLET SALAD

Serves 4

1 CUP SHREDDED BUTTER
LEAF LETTUCE

1/4 CUP DICED SHALLOTS

1/4 CUP DICED PLUM TOMATOES

2 TABLESPOONS PINE NUTS

PETALS FROM 12 VIOLETS

6 FRESH MINT LEAVES,
FOR GARNISH

Dressing

1/8 CUP OLIVE OIL

1/8 CUP WHITE WINE VINEGAR

1 TABLESPOONS CHOPPED
FRESH PARSLEY

1/4 CUP RASPBERRIES

During the Middle Ages, salad was eaten and enjoyed but not to excess. Eating too much salad was considered an unseemly behavior. People of this era partook of heavy foods that could sustain them through rough seasonal weather. Only people who couldn't afford savory, well-seasoned foods would be reduced to eating bland lettuce. Also according to aristocratic taste, a lavish, flavorful dressing had to be mixed in the salad.

Another inventive way people ate their salads, especially if they couldn't afford expensive herbs and spices, was to add fresh flowers. The flowers' aromatic extract enhanced the flavor, and the bright colors embellished the dish. Besides violets, other herbs and flowers used in medieval salads included parsley, watercress, primrose buds, daisies, dandelions, rocket, red nettles, borage flowers, red fennel, and chickweed.

Mix the lettuce, shallots, tomatoes, and nuts in a bowl.

To make the dressing, combine the oil, vinegar, parsley, and raspberries in a small bowl. Stir well. Mix the dressing into the salad and toss.

Just before serving, add the violet petals. Garnish with mint leaves.

Deva Saffron Bread

Serves 10

3/4 CUP WARM MILK

1 (1/4-OUNCE) PACKAGE
ACTIVE DRY YEAST

1 TEASPOON GRANULATED SUGAR

1/4 TEASPOON SAFFRON STRANDS

1/2 CUP BOILING WATER

3 1/2 CUPS ALL-PURPOSE FLOUR

1 CUP BUTTER, SOFTENED

1/2 CUP SUPERFINE SUGAR

1/2 CUP RAISINS

1/2 CUP DRIED CRANBERRIES

1/2 CUP CHOPPED CANDIED
ORANGE PEEL

1 TEASPOON MINCED
FRESH THYME

In the Middle Ages, spices were a symbol of status and prosperity. Aristocrats' meals were ordinarily heavily spiced, and saffron was especially favored. The attractive, bright yellow was used to color a variety of dishes.

It is believed that Welsh devas, also known as faeries, thrived on saffron. A twelfth-century story by Giraldus Cambrensis tells of a boy who was taken to a faery palace and found that the whole faery court ate nothing but saffron and milk.

The saffron crocus was first found in Greece and Asia Minor. Later, medieval people found that they could grow the flower closer to home. Spain, Italy, and England all produced large quantities of saffron.

Pour the milk into a bowl and dissolve the yeast and the sugar in it. Let stand in a warm place for approximately 10 minutes, until foaming. Steep the saffron in the boiling water for several minutes, then let the mixture cool.

Sift the flour into a large bowl. In a small bowl, cream the butter and sugar. Then add raisins, cranberries, orange peel, and thyme, mixing well. Gradually add the flour.

Strain the saffron mixture. Add the yeast mixture and saffron liquid to the flour mixture. Mix with a wooden spoon until smooth; it should look like a very thick batter.

Preheat the oven to 375°F. Pour the batter into a greased and lined 10-inch round cake pan. Cover with a damp cloth and leave in a warm place for about 1 hour, until the mixture rises to the top of the pan. Bake the bread for 1 hour. Let it cool in the pan.

Slice and serve with butter.

Note: When buying saffron, try to obtain strands (stamens) rather than powder—you can then be sure that you are getting the real thing. Before pounding or soaking saffron strands for use in a recipe, dry them for a few minutes in a low oven in the sun; they will then more readily attain their gorgeous regal color.

Elder Flower Sweet Bread

Serves 12

1 LARGE EGG

1 TEASPOON ORANGE
BLOSSOM EXTRACT

1/3 CUP HONEY

2 TABLESPOONS BRANDY

1 CUP SELF-RISING FLOUR

1/4 TEASPOON GROUND CINNAMON

2 CUPS ELDER FLOWER HEADS,
FRESHLY PICKED AND CLEANED

2 MINT LEAVES, FINELY CHOPPED

JUICE OF 1 LEMON, FOR GARNISH

SWEET CREAM, FOR GARNISH

Elder was so widely used by European gypsies that this favorite remedy earned the title "the medicine chest of the country people." In the Middle Ages, elder branches were hollowed out to make flutes and whistles. The music drifted over many a field, moor, and valley. Today many people use all parts of this plant for herbal baths, cooling teas, lotions, and wine.

As you prepare this dish, meditate on the wanderlust of the gypsy within you. See yourself in an exotic land anticipating the festival of the Spring Equinox. Imagine the sights your eyes will feast on and the smells to which your nose will be privy. How will you be dressed? Are you experiencing a past life, a distant country, or a place in your own town that you have left unexplored for too long? Within our world, there is much to delight in, and even seeing the old and familiar with new eyes can allow a striking experience that can expand your outlook and understanding.

Mix the egg, orange extract, honey, and brandy in a bowl. Stir in the flour and cinnamon. The batter should resemble slightly thick pancake batter. If the batter is too thin, add a little more flour; too thick, add more brandy or orange blossom extract. Fold in the elder flower heads and mint leaves.

Heat the griddle, then drop a sprinkle of water on it. If the water dances, the griddle is ready. Add oil to the griddle and heat. Fry the batter like pancakes on the hot griddle (or drop by the teaspoon into a deep fat fryer and fry until golden brown).

Sprinkle with some orange blossom extract and the juice of a lemon, or top with fresh sweet cream.

Note: If you are not using self-rising flour, add 1 teaspoon baking powder and 1/2 teaspoon salt to all-purpose flour.

Orange blossom extract can be bought where liquor is sold.

"Be Sweet" Honey Cakes

6 cakes

1/2 CUP RIESLING OR OTHER
SWEET WHITE WINE

1 LARGE EGG

2/3 CUP ALL-PURPOSE FLOUR

1/8 TEASPOON GROUND CINNAMON

DASH OF SALT

2 TABLESPOONS
GRANULATED SUGAR

1 CUP HONEY

1/8 TEASPOON GRATED NUTMEG

During the Middle Ages, honey cakes were left in the garden to please faery visitors. Faeries are known to love sweet dishes, especially those made with honey. Honey is an elixir for the nature devas, and for them it is served with every dish. In their land, it is believed that honey brings out the romantic nature due to its sweetness.

By all means, leave something for the faeries to eat. Faeries are quite active in Ostara, the Spring Equinox, when they come to collect a portion of the sabbat feast. If they are denied their treats, they will cause much havoc until Summer Solstice, when the payment of food should be doubled to make amends. If they are again ignored, you might as well move, because their reign of havoc will continue until next Spring Equinox.

Beat the wine and egg in a bowl. In a small bowl, combine the flour, cinnamon, salt, and sugar. Add the flour mixture to the egg mixture. Mix until well blended. Let stand for 30 minutes. Combine the honey and nutmeg in a small bowl.

Heat 1/2 inch of oil in a skillet until hot, but not smoking. Drop the batter into the oil 1 tablespoon at a time; fry until golden brown. Drain on paper towels.

Serve cakes with honey mixture, for dipping.

Hot Cross Buns

This commonly baked dish is included in many Ostara celebrations. The roundness of the bun, which is intersected with a perfect equilateral cross, is symbolic of the flawless balance achieved at this time, when night and day enjoy equal status.

This holiday marks the time when we find ourselves in the balance between light and dark, the presence of the God is felt in the radiance of the sun warming our faces and the Goddess is also seen in the blossoming flowers and burgeoning new growth. If your life is not already in balance, try this spell to reestablish your equilibrium.

Begin at your altar. Put away or otherwise recycle the symbolic talismans or decorations from the past holiday. Gather spring flowers, decorative eggs, anything green, incense, and three candles ahead of time. Carefully, thoughtfully, and symmetrically, place your items on your altar, being cautious to balance the feminine and male energies inherent in each piece. Light one candle. Say

> *To the God I freely give my woes.*
> *In turn, I reap strength to fight my foes.*

Light the second candle. Say

> *I walk with the Mother and release*
> *Control to Her who gives me peace.*

Light the third candle. Say

> *I now feel the balance in my life.*
> *With the moon's waxing and waning,*
> *I flow with nature and banish strife.*

Serves 12

---

3 CUPS ALL-PURPOSE FLOUR

1/4 CUP GRAHAM FLOUR

1/4 CUP FIRMLY PACKED LIGHT
BROWN SUGAR

1 TEASPOON SALT

1 TEASPOON GROUND CINNAMON

1/2 TEASPOON GRATED NUTMEG

1/4 TEASPOON GROUND GINGER

1 CUP WARM WATER

1 (1/4-OUNCE) PACKAGE
ACTIVE DRY YEAST

2 LARGE EGGS, 1 SEPARATED

4 TABLESPOONS BUTTER,
SOFTENED

1 TEASPOON WATER

1 TEASPOON GRANULATED SUGAR

Icing

2 CUPS CONFECTIONERS' SUGAR

1 TABLESPOON MILK

2 CUPS FRESHLY SQUEEZED
ORANGE JUICE

Visualize the pieces of your life falling back into place and the equilibrium being reestablished. Say

Balance is restored unto me.
So Mote it Be.
This I make true.
Three times three times three.

In a large bowl, mix 1 cup of the all-purpose flour, the graham flour, brown sugar, salt, cinnamon, nutmeg, and ginger. Blend the warm water and yeast. Let stand for 5 to 10 minutes, until foaming. In this order, stir the following items into the yeast mixture: spiced flour mixture, 1 egg, 1 egg yolk, and butter. Gradually add the remaining 2 cups of the all-purpose flour, mixing well. Scrape the dough down. Cover with a clean cotton kitchen towel and let rise for 45 to 60 minutes, or until doubled in size.

Punch down the dough. Turn the dough out onto a lightly floured surface. Toss the dough until it's smooth and no longer sticky. Roll the dough out to 1 inch thick. Cut into rounds with a floured water glass. Cover and let rise for 30 to 35 minutes.

Preheat the oven to 375°F. Combine egg white, 1 teaspoon of water, and sugar. Brush the buns with the glaze. Bake for 15 to 18 minutes.

To make the icing, combine the ingredients in a small bowl. After the buns have cooled, make a cross on top of each bun with the icing.

White Chocolate Mousse in Tulip Cups

Serves 6 to 8

4 OUNCES WHITE CHOCOLATE

1/2 CUP SWEET BUTTER

2 EGG YOLKS

3 TABLESPOONS FRANGELICO
LIQUEUR

3 EGG WHITES, AT ROOM
TEMPERATURE

1/2 TEASPOON CREAM OF TARTAR

6 TO 8 TULIPS, RINSED AND DRIED

1/4 TEASPOON NUTMEG, GRATED

SPRING FLOWERS, FOR GARNISH

Tulips have been cultivated for a thousand years, originating in Persia or, according to some sources, Turkey. Approximately 150 varieties of tulips grow in the wild, especially in cold, mountainous regions. The name "tulip" comes from the headdress worn by many Middle Eastern peoples we know as a "turban" or taliban.

In the years 1636 and 1637, tulipmania ruled in the Netherlands. Tulips were a symbol of wealth and status and were traded like currency. A bed of tulips could buy a small house. Some highly prized varieties were so valuable that a single bulb could be traded for a house, its contents, and all the surrounding land. The most coveted tulips had breaks or stripes in their coloration, the result of a virus transferred by aphids, which made their appearance unpredictable. By 1638 the tulip market became saturated and collapsed, with repercussions similar to the stock market crash in the United States in 1929.

Tulips represent fame and perfect love, but their symbolic meaning changes according to the color of the blooms. Red tulips mean "Believe me" and are a declaration of love. Variegated tulips mean "You have beautiful eyes." Yellow tulips mean "There's sunshine in your smile." And cream-colored tulips mean "I will love you forever." This recipe works best with cream-colored tulips.

In the top of a double boiler, melt the chocolate until smooth. Stir in the butter, remove from the heat, and allow to cool for a few minutes. Stir in the egg yolks, one at a time, then add the Frangelico. Set aside.

In a bowl, beat the egg whites with the cream of tartar until fairly stiff. Using a spatula, carefully fold the chocolate mixture into the beaten egg whites. Refrigerate for 10 to 15 minutes.

Carefully pull open the tulip petals and, using a small pair of scissors, remove the pistil, stamen, and stem. Remove the mousse from the refrigerator and mound 1 to 2 tablespoons of the mousse into pudding cups. Gently nestle a tulip blossom into each mound of mousse. Then carefully fill each tulip to three-quarters full with the remaining mousse. Sprinkle with the nutmeg. Garnish with spring flowers.

Ostara Pineapple Punch

Serves 18 to 20

1 CUP GRANULATED SUGAR

1 CUP WATER

1 (42-OUNCE) CAN PINEAPPLE
JUICE

2 (6-OUNCE) CANS FROZEN
LEMONADE

2 QUARTS (2 LITERS) GINGER ALE

stara is the goddess of fertility and creation. Ostara is connected to wetness and moisture. Before our creation we were submerged in liquid, a protective substance that provided warmth and nourishment. When we cast circles, we pour liquids onto Mother Earth to symbolically honor Mother Ocean and her nurturing aspects.

Rabbits are fertile creatures, and as they give birth in the spring, they make a wonderful companion for Ostara. Rabbit is the companion, server, and messenger for Ostara. Rabbit calls forth fears, forcing us to confront them, either learning from them or becoming consumed by them. Rabbit medicine embodies the saying "What you resist persists." Whatever you ask for or concentrate on, you will get in spadefuls with Rabbit's help. Since obstacles are opportunities for growth, Rabbit guides us and points to the need to address and face our fears.

As you partake of this drink, take a moment to relax. If it coincides with your belief system, either rub a rabbit's foot or other item with rabbit fur during this rite. Get comfortable and connect with Spirit. Feel the Mother of all surrounding you with Her love. You are protected in the most complete way possible. Now concentrate on your deepest fear. Recognize that you have the ability to step forward and see beyond the fear to the lesson that is being offered. As you wash down this drink, feel the strength coursing through your body. Say

I am strong enough.
I possess the strength of the God.
I possess the endurance of the Goddess.
I call upon all who have come before me.
I can conquer my fears.
And make my weaknesses my greatest strengths.

In a saucepan, make a sugar syrup by mixing the sugar and water. Bring to a boil and stir until the sugar melts, approximately 2 minutes. Add the juice, lemonade, and ginger ale, stirring well. Serve chilled.

DANDELION WINE

Traditionally in Europe and America, fresh dandelions have been a favorite ingredient in springtime tonics. The dandelion has been around since ancient times and is widely known for its multiple uses, including as a laxative and for treating diabetes, liver diseases, pancreas ailments, anemic conditions, and kidney and bladder infections. It is also added to coffee to thwart its detrimental effects.

The dandelion is a favorite of young children as well. Known as a weed to many a gardener, it is known to children and the young at heart as a wish maker once its petals have turned from yellow to delicate white tufts. In a field or even your backyard, look for the light puffballs and make a wish with a light heart, imagining yourself as free as you were meant to be.

During the Middle Ages, dandelion wine was a favorite treat, especially made for the Spring Equinox festivities. Here's a toast from Thomas D'Urfey you can use as you clink glasses with friends and guests alike.

> *Drinking will make a man quaff,*
> *Quaffing will make a man sing,*
> *Singing will make a man laugh,*
> *And laughing doth long life bring.*

About 1 gallon

8 CUPS FRESH DANDELION
FLOWER HEADS

1 LEMON, THINLY SLICED

1 TANGELO, THINLY SLICED

1 SMALL ORANGE, THINLY SLICED

1 BREAD SLICE, TOASTED

1 GALLON BOILING WATER

6 CUPS GRANULATED SUGAR

1 OUNCE FRESH YEAST

Place the dandelion flower heads in a large bowl. Add the orange, tangelo, and lemon to the flower heads. Pour the boiling water over the flower-head mixture, stirring well. Cover the bowl tightly; let stand for 10 days, stirring daily.

Strain the liquid into another bowl, and stir in the sugar until it is dissolved. Spread the yeast on a piece of toast and float it on top of the liquid. Cover the bowl and leave it in a dry, cool place for another 3 days, stirring daily.

Remove the toast and strain again. Pour the wine into a gallon container, making sure to leave space at the top of the container for the fermenting process. Cover the bottleneck with a balloon. When the balloon goes limp, the wine is done fermenting, which will take approximately 3 months.

Cork loosely. Keep in a refrigerator for 2 weeks. Place a surgical or other sterile tube into the wine, stopped 1 inch above the sediment. Siphon off the wine into another gallon container, leaving the sediment in the original bottle. Discard the sediment.

Note: As always, be sure to pick the dandelions on a sunny day. Keep just the heads until you have two 1-quart jugs full. Discard the stems and leaves, possibly in a compost heap. Lightly but thoroughly wash the flower heads.

BELTANE

Beltane (also known as May Day, Rood Day, Rudemas, and Walpurgisnacht) is celebrated on May Eve and May 1.

Beltane, a frivolous, lusty sabbat, is dedicated to fertility and the returning of the sun. A maypole crowned with wild flowers and multicolored ribbons is the center of the dance. As weaving and plaiting are common practices of Beltane, you are invited to dance around the maypole and intertwine the ribbons while you sing songs. This dance symbolizes the union or marriage of the Goddess and her Consort; the joining of two to form a third entity. Try to celebrate near a forest or living tree.

Faeries are known to be quite active during Beltane. It is important to pay heed to nature's devas. Pan is also remembered with great reverence, as He is yet another incarnation of the Horned One.

Other traditions to celebrate this sabbat include making small wedding gifts for the Goddess and God, such as a string of beads, potpourri bags, or flower garlands to hang from a tree; a basket of flowers at a neighbor's doorstep, or hearth; bonfires; or flower-and-ribbon hair wreaths known as chaplets (in honor of Flora, the Roman goddess of flowers).

Herbs and flowers associated with Beltane include almond, angelica, ash tree, bluebell, cinquefoil, daisy, frankincense, hawthorn, honeysuckle, ivy, lilac, marigold, meadowsweet, primrose, rose, satyrion root (also known as orchis), Saint John's wort, woodruff, and yellow cowslips.

Traditional foods of Beltane include Beltane cakes (round oatmeal or barleycakes), doughnuts, cookies, fresh fruit (usually red fruits, such as raspberries or cherries), herbal salads, honey, marigold custard, mead, vanilla ice cream, and wine punch.

Ares' Asparagus Soup

Serves 4 to 6

1 CUP CHOPPED CHIVES

1 TABLESPOON BUTTER

1 CUBE VEGETABLE BOUILLON

3 TO 4 RUSSET POTATOES, PEELED
AND CUBED

12 SPEARS ASPARAGUS, CHOPPED
INTO 1-INCH PIECES

SALT AND PEPPER

The Doctrine of Signatures, a philosophy shared by herbalists dating back to the Middle Ages, states that one can determine God's purpose for a plant from the color of its flowers or roots, the shape of its leaves, the place where it grows, or what it resembles. Because asparagus looks similar to the male genitalia, it was thought to be an aphrodisiac. This recipe, a perfect side dish for any Beltane celebration, is linked to Ares, the virile Greek god of war, to invoke dynamic passion and raw sensuality. He was, after all, Aphrodite's favorite lover.

Beltane rituals, such as the May Pole dance, were performed to honor or invoke fertility—both human and agricultural. Life was precarious for our ancestors, and healthy children and abundant crops were never taken for granted. Literal and symbolic veneration for the act of procreation was a natural part of life. Beltane revelers drank mead, feasted on their newly harvested bounty, and celebrated long into the evening, eventually falling into each other's arms for a raucous night of copulation.

This dish, from Dreim Diva, Melinda Rodriguez, can help you experience the sacredness inherent in sexuality. With reverent intention for the playful and lusty Beltane holiday, say this chant three times while you prepare the meal, and repeat it again as you serve it.

I summon and invoke the bold and virile Aries
The playful, unencumbered sentiment of faeries
The liberation from a cold, barren winter's end,
To practice sex as sacred is what I intend.

In a small sauté pan, sauté the chives in the butter for 1 to 2 minutes. Transfer to a large pot. Add about 4 to 6 cups of water, depending on your preference for thicker or thinner soup. Add the bouillon cube, and bring to a boil. Add the potatoes and asparagus, adding water as needed, and reduce the heat to medium. Simmer until the potatoes are soft. Transfer to a food processor or blender. Blend until smooth. Salt and pepper to taste.

SCRUMPTIOUS SAGE SOUP

Serves 4

8 OUNCES OF PENNE, BOWTIE, OR
SHELL PASTA

2 TABLESPOONS OLIVE OIL

1 MEDIUM ONION, CHOPPED FINE,
OR 1 CUP CELERY, CHOPPED FINE,
OR MIXTURE

2 CLOVES GARLIC, CHOPPED

2 CARROTS, ROUGHLY CHOPPED

1 (16-OUNCE) CAN WHITE BEANS,
DRAINED AND RINSED

1 CUP VEGETABLE BROTH

2 TEASPOONS FRESH GARDEN
SAGE, CHOPPED

1/4 CUP SUNDRIED TOMATOES,
CHOPPED

1/4 TEASPOON SALT

2 TABLESPOONS FRESHLY
SQUEEZED LEMON JUICE

1/2 CUP PARMESAN CHEESE

3 TABLESPOONS CHOPPED PARSLEY

This recipe calls for Garden Sage (*Salvia officinalis*). The name *salvia* originates from the Latin word *salvere*, meaning to be in good health, to cure, to save. So it's no surprise that sage is an important in dishes that promote good health and well-being. Taking well-being to the next level would be to include a healthy amount of pleasure in your life. Hedonism is the state of pure pleasure and the dominant mood of the Beltane holiday. Ancient pagans celebrated that the worst of the winter season was behind them with wild abandon. Modern pagans enjoy the ephemeral feeling of surrender meeting the physical experience of ecstasy.

We can stop ourselves from experiencing hedonism for a variety of reasons: denying the flesh may appear to be more spiritual; rising above base impulses may seem more sophisticated; or perhaps the "crab" theory applies—those who are immersed in victim mentality cannot stand to see another's pleasure so exert pressure on others to be as miserable as the rest.

But at Beltane, all are invited to yield to the sensory pleasures, to be overtaken by them. During the week before Beltane, make a daily list of five things for which you are grateful and share them with a friend or family each day. Allow joy, contentment, and pleasure to suffuse this period of time; banish feelings of shame or guilt. Have a little old-fashioned feral fun!

Bring water to a boil. Cook the pasta until tender 7 to 10 minutes. Meanwhile, prepare sauce: heat oil in a large skillet over medium heat. Add onion and cook, stirring frequently, until onion is softened—about 5 minutes. Add garlic and cook for 1 minute. Add carrots, stirring occasionally for 5 minutes. Add beans, broth, sage, sundried tomatoes, and salt; cook 5 minutes, mashing about one-quarter of the beans with wood spoon against the side of the skillet—this will be your "sauce." Add lemon juice, cook 2 minutes. Add parmesan and parsley. Drain pasta, add to skillet and mix. Serve immediately with more grated parmesan cheese.

Beltane Oatcake

8 cakes

2 TABLESPOONS VEGETABLE
SHORTENING

1/3 CUP BOILING WATER

3 CUPS ROLLED OATS

1 TEASPOON MINCED FRESH SAGE

1/4 TEASPOON BAKING SODA

1/2 TEASPOON SALT

atcakes are part of the Beltane ceremony. Their roundness is symbolic of the life-giving sun whose return is marked by this festive sabbat. Traditionally, during Beltane a huge bonfire is kept going all night long. Pieces of the cake are thrown into the fire as an offering to the protective deities.

Participate in this ancient custom by casting the oatcakes into an outside bonfire or even your fireplace. Begin by blessing these cakes. Say a prayer of gratitude, giving thanks to the Goddess and God for their abundance. Pass around the cake in a clockwise direction. Invite each of your guests to take a piece of the cake. Say

> *We are each a part of the joyous circle of love.*
> *As we cast the bread into the fire,*
> *We fuse together into the One Being,*
> *That always was and always will be.*

Recommend to your guests that they remember the joy in their heart as they experience the gaiety of the season.

Preheat the oven to 350°F. In a small pan, heat the shortening and water, until the shortening has melted. Remove from heat and let cool.

Mix the oats, sage, baking soda, and salt together in a bowl. Mix the cooled liquid and the oat mixture, adding water, if necessary, to maintain a doughlike consistency.

Pat the dough into a circle, about 8 inches in diameter. Place on an ungreased baking sheet. Bake for about 40 minutes.

Cut into 8 wedges, then leave to cool on a wire rack.

Zucchini-Chocolate Muffins

Although chocolate was not discovered until the end of the Middle Ages, this delectable sweet soon became a beloved treat of the elite and is a favorite among children. One ritual that includes children, as well as uses the gifts of nature, is the making of flower baskets. Everything in nature is sacred. A good way to utilize all parts of the zucchini plant in this recipe is to incorporate the flower in to your basket.

You will need construction paper, scissors or a hole punch, pipe cleaners, fresh flowers, colored markers, and either tape, staples, or glue. Fold each side of the paper about 1¹/₂ inches toward the center. Flatten the paper. Pinch each corner inward to lift up two perpendicular sides. Crease the excess paper and fold to the left, securing with tape, staples, or glue. On the longer sides, write your holiday greetings. Make a hole in the center of each shorter side, about 1 inch from the bottom. From the inside, poke one pipe cleaner through the hole about 2 inches. Bend the pipe cleaner, forming a large "L," and wrap the small end of the pipe cleaner back around itself. This will be the handle. Place flowers from the zucchini plant or fresh flowers in the basket.

You can also make flowers with the pipe cleaners, using green ones for the stem and leaves and multicolored ones for the flower heads. Arrange two green pipe cleaners in an equilateral cross, bending one around the other several times to secure it. Use this pipe cleaner to form oval-shaped or pointy leaves. Bend the tip of the stem around the center of another color of pipe cleaner. To make a tulip, bend the pipe cleaner to form a U, then, with each side of the pipe cleaner, form a V. Attach at the center. To make a daisy, form an infinity or figure-eight shape with each side of the pipe cleaner and attach at the center. This gives you a creative start. Now you can design your own flowers.

Continues on next page

ZUCCHINI-CHOCOLATE MUFFINS, continued

1 dozen muffins

1¹/₃ CUPS ALL-PURPOSE FLOUR

1 CUP GRANULATED SUGAR

¹/₂ CUP UNSWEETENED
COCOA POWDER

2¹/₂ TEASPOONS BAKING POWDER

¹/₂ TEASPOON BAKING SODA

¹/₂ TEASPOON SALT

¹/₂ CUP LOWFAT SOUR CREAM

1 LARGE EGG

2 TABLESPOONS VEGETABLE OIL

2 TEASPOONS VANILLA EXTRACT

1¹/₂ CUPS LOOSELY PACKED
SHREDDED ZUCCHINI
(SEE VARIATION)

When your basket is ready, carry it to your neighbor's house. As children, we would place the baskets on the doormat, ring the doorbell, then run and hide. We gained impish delight in peering around the bushes to watch our neighbor's expression change from disappointment to surprise and delight at the beautiful springtime flowers. This playful "dingdong ditching" provides a memorable childhood experience that combines the spirit of giving with the mischievous side of Beltane.

Preheat the oven to 400°F. In a large bowl, stir together the flour, sugar, cocoa, baking powder, baking soda, and salt. In a small bowl, mix the sour cream, egg, oil, and vanilla. Add the zucchini, being careful not to overmix. Stir the sour cream mixture carefully into the dry ingredients.

Fill each cup of a muffin pan three-fourths full with the batter. Bake for 20 minutes.

Variation
You can substitute ¹/₂ cup of applesauce for ¹/₂ cup of the zucchini for a different taste. That said, these muffins are worth every calorie.

Wild Rose Faery Jam

4 cups

2 CUPS WATER

2 CUPS FRAGRANT ROSE PETALS,
WHITE BASES REMOVED

1 (1³/4 OUNCE) PACKAGE
POWDERED PECTIN

2¹/2 CUPS SUPERFINE SUGAR

¹/8 CUP FRESHLY SQUEEZED
LEMON JUICE

1³/4 TABLESPOONS ROSE WATER
(PAGE 131)

Faeries run freely during the Beltane sabbat, as well as midsummer. The roses in this jam are a perfect and delicate treat to honor the faeries and can be eaten over Beltane oatcakes.

The rose is a symbol of the Goddess. The growth of the rose illustrates the path from maiden, to mother, to crone, as it grows from bud, to full bloom, to fallen, faded petals. The rose also shows that with each death it grows back stronger and more vital. This is symbolic of how, when we face and overcome obstacles or shed negativity, we become powerful and closer to the Divine Source. The rose has long been admired for its delicate beauty and is favored by many, including in the faery realm, where the deva of this flower reigns as royalty. You may choose to repeat this saying as you make this jam.

With gentle patience, we await Her arrival.
Her timeless beauty, we are soon to marvel.
Her regal essence scents the air of June.
Blossoms yet to bud will unfold and bloom.
Her quiet knowledge and bliss that resides within,
Are gifts from rose, and for you to take in.

In a large saucepan, bring the water to a boil. Decrease heat to the simmering point and add the rose petals. Simmer for 5 minutes, until petals are pliable. Whisk in the pectin and bring to a boil over high heat stirring frequently. Add the sugar and lemon juice. Bring back to a boil. Decrease heat and simmer for 30 minutes. Stir until the sugar has dissolved and the mixture begins to thicken. Add the rose water. Let stand, until foaming. Skim foam.

To test for doneness, place a spoonful of the jam on a cold saucer. Allow the mixture to cool, then gently press on the surface; if it wrinkles, it is ready. Pour into sterilized jars. Store in the refrigerator; jam will keep up to two months.

ANGEL NOODLES IN FAERY BUTTER

Serves 8

4 HARD-BOILED EGG YOLKS

1/2 CUP GRANULATED SUGAR

1/2 CUP UNSALTED BUTTER, SOFTENED

2 TEASPOONS MINCED FRESH ROSEMARY

2 TEASPOONS MINCED FRESH SWEET BASIL

2 TABLESPOONS ROSE WATER (PAGE 131)

16 OUNCES ANGEL-HAIR PASTA

1 ORANGE, SLICED, FOR GARNISH

 ith its vibrant color and springtime scene, this noodle entrée encourages thoughts of faery kinship, childlike energy, nature's angelic realm, lighthearted fun, and friendship. As you make this dish, attune yourself to nature's devas—nature's spirits or faeries, also known as the spirits of the trees and plants.

Invite your favorite faery to cook with you. See if they will reveal their names. Often faeries, just like angels, are anxiously waiting to be asked before they can come and play with you. Feel their impish, happy energy dance around you. If you honor the spiritual essence in every living plant, flower, and tree, soon you will find yourself giggling for no apparent reason. For the first time, you may notice the smallest drop of dew on a rose as the sun kisses it good morning. A sense of calm protection comes when you make friends with the faeries.

In a small bowl, beat together the egg yolks, sugar, butter, rosemary, basil, and rose water. Mix until smooth.

Boil water. Cook the pasta for 12 to 14 minutes, until al dente or to taste. Drain the noodles. Combine the egg-yolk mixture with the pasta. To achieve a golden-yellow color, add more butter to the hot noodles.

Garnish with orange slices.

Ham and Calendula Finger Sandwiches

10 to 12 sandwiches

1 (8-OUNCE) PACKAGE CREAM
CHEESE, AT ROOM TEMPERATURE

2 TABLESPOONS LOWFAT
MAYONNAISE

1 TABLESPOONS HORSERADISH

3 TEASPOONS FRESHLY SQUEEZED
LEMON JUICE

2 TABLESPOONS SWEET
PICKLE RELISH

1 TART APPLE, PEELED, CORED,
AND FINELY DICED

1 CUP CALENDULA PETALS PLUS
EXTRA, FOR GARNISH

1 HERBED FLATBREAD (PAGE 117)

1 CUP VERY THINLY SLICED HAM

PARSLEY, FOR GARNISH

Calendula is easy to find and grow in a variety of climates. The flower is available at local nurseries and can be obtained quite easily during Beltane. It is a mild herb and has been used since the Middle Ages for its many healing properties: salving wounds, soothing skin rashes, and bee stings; treating conjunctivitis, toothaches, and ulcers; and breaking fevers.

I (Jamie) prepared this dish for my second child's naming ceremony. Born on the Spring Equinox, he was already demonstrating impish behavior of the sprite he was soon to become. As part of the ceremony, we purchased an orange tree. Each guest was asked to bring a stone or gem as a gift for the babe. After setting circle, offering gifts to Goddess and God, and purifying the participants, we placed a handful of dirt at the bottom of a very large pot. Then I placed my child's placenta on the dirt. Next, we planted the tree. Each guest stepped forward, added a handful of dirt, and put their stone in, along with casting their greatest wish for the baby's future. We circled clockwise three times, and when we reached our original places, all proclaimed his full name, calling his mind, spirit, and body into this mundane, earthly world. Then we feasted on my favorite Beltane desserts, leaving the sweetest for the faeries, of course.

Mix the cheese, mayonnaise, horseradish, lemon juice, and pickle relish in a bowl. Gently stir in the apple and calendula petals. With the back of a spoon or spatula, spread the mixture over the bread. Cover the spread with a single layer of ham slices. Cut into squares immediately or wrap tightly in plastic wrap and chill until serving. Garnish the serving dish with parsley and calendula petals.

Note: Be certain to use Calendula officinalis, also known as Pot Marigold, and not common Marigold (Tagetes), which is toxic.

Divine Chicken Skewers

Serves 6

Marinade

1/2 CUP PLAIN LOWFAT YOGURT

1 ONION, QUARTERED

3 LARGE CLOVES GARLIC, CHOPPED

2 TABLESPOONS FRESHLY
SQUEEZED LEMON JUICE

1-INCH PIECE FRESH GINGER,
PEELED AND CHOPPED

2 TEASPOONS VEGETABLE OIL

3/4 TEASPOON GROUND CINNAMON

1/2 TEASPOON ALLSPICE

1/2 TEASPOON GROUND TURMERIC

1/4 TEASPOON GROUND
RED PEPPER

SALT AND PEPPER

Chicken was the most prevalent meat in the Middle Ages. Try preparing this modern recipe while listening to soothing music. Throughout the ages, cooks have used music to inspire them and to set a mood or intended atmosphere. Music will help you float away to that place where you move in perfect rhythm with the Mother.

Match your music to the mood you want to create at mealtime. Dance as you quarter, mince, and peel. Hum or sing along as you thread each piece of food onto the skewers. Imagine each ingredient as a gift for your friends and family. What will you offer them today?

To make the marinade, combine the ingredients and purée in a blender until smooth.

Place the chicken in a bowl. Pour the marinade over the chicken and toss to coat well. Refrigerate, covered, for 6 hours (or overnight).

Prepare a medium-hot grill. Thread the chicken and bell peppers onto skewers. Cook for 5 to 6 minutes. Carefully thread 1 to 2 cherry tomatoes onto each hot skewer. Cook the other sides of the skewers until the chicken is cooked through and brown, about 6 minutes.

Serve over rice.

Chicken

2 POUNDS BONELESS,
SKINLESS CHICKEN BREASTS,
CUT INTO 1³/₄-INCH CUBES

2 GREEN BELL PEPPERS, SEEDED,
CUT INTO 1-INCH PIECES

1 PINT CHERRY TOMATOES

RICE, COOKED, ENOUGH
FOR 6 SERVINGS

GRIDDLE AHI WITH HERBS

The peppercorn in this dish has long been known as a catalyst to change work situations for those who practice Santeria. Many of us find ourselves from time to time in search of a new job or better position. Often we feel stressed out, underappreciated, underpaid, or otherwise displaced. Beltane is a good time for reflection on your life's work. First, we must come to terms with the fact that we are always exactly where we need to be for the necessary lessons we were born to learn. There is a Divine reason for your current job. It is your assignment to see that; otherwise it will be difficult for you to move forward. Often the Goddess withholds further progress until harmony has been established in the present situation. If you are having difficulty seeing the blessing or gift offered in your current job, bless it the best you can, mentally anointing every aspect of it with love. Any effort counts if you do it with sincerity, and your efforts will be rewarded.

We sometimes become stuck or stagnant in our employment and need a push to move forward. Perhaps we have not made it absolutely clear to the Universe that we are ready for a change. To remedy this, after you prepare this dish, take several peppercorns or the whole container to work with you.

Shake the peppercorns under your workstation, imagining the perfect job for you, specifically outlining every detail of your new position (for example, an increase in salary, flexibility, a better mentor/boss, compatible coworkers, or whatever else would satisfy your needs and desires. Say

> I am now manifesting the perfect job for me.
> In my new position I have (fill in the positive aspects).
> I am making (fill in the number) dollars a year.
> I am content.
> This or better I am manifesting right now.

Serves 6

_____

6 (6-OUNCE) FRESH AHI FILLETS

6 SPRIGS PARSLEY

6 TEASPOONS CHOPPED FRESH
MINT LEAVES

1/4 CUP CHOPPED FRESH
THYME LEAVES

4 TEASPOONS CHOPPED FRESH
SAGE LEAVES

1 1/2 TEASPOONS COARSE SEA SALT
OR REGULAR SALT

1/3 CUP UNSALTED BUTTER,
SOFTENED

FRESHLY GROUND PEPPERCORNS
(ABOUT 6 TO 9 GRINDS)

We include that last line to make sure that in this illimitable world you do not draw boundaries and restrict yourself from the abundance that is your Divine right. The Goddess has a great future planned for you.

⁂

Make an incision in each fillet and tuck one sprig of parsley inside each fish fillet. In a small bowl, mix the mint, thyme, sage, salt, and butter. Generously coat the fish on each side with the herb mixture.

Griddle, barbecue, or grill (see note) the fish for 4 to 5 minutes on each side until the skin is well browned and the meat is flaking. Grind the peppercorns onto the fish. Baste occasionally with the butter, which runs off. To test for doneness, place a fork in the thickest part of the fish. Gently twist the fork; when the fish flakes easily, it is ready.

Serve immediately with fresh bread and salad or green vegetable.

Note: Be sure to scrape your grill, then wipe it with a cloth saturated in vegetable oil.

MEAD

Serves 4

1 GALLON WATER

4 POUNDS HONEY

6 WHOLE CLOVES

2 STICKS CINNAMON

PEEL OF 1 LEMON

JUICE OF 1 LEMON

1 TEASPOON ACTIVE DRY YEAST

¼ CUP WARM WATER

In accordance with this raucous, feisty sabbat, mead is often included with vociferous drinking and the exuberant merriment enjoyed during the Beltane celebration. Beltane is the time when we can finally let our hair down and be one with the wild and rambunctious side of ourselves. The wind tingles with excitement. Faeries prance around. You might even find the hoofprints of Pan on your lawn the next day. Let us dance as much as we can all day and laugh for just as long. This holiday is made for fun. Many a pagan drank himself to oblivion, just as this toast form the 1600s suggests:

(Mead's) a strong wrestler,
Flings all it hath met;
And makes the ground slippery,
Though it not be wet.

In a large, nonreactive pot, combine the water, honey, cloves, cinnamon, and lemon peel and juice. Boil for 30 minutes.

Blend the yeast into the warm water. Let stand for 5 to 10 minutes, until foaming.

Strain the honey mixture into an earthenware or heavy ceramic jug that will hold it with a little room to spare. When it is cooled, add the yeast. Cover the neck of the jug with a balloon. Allow to ferment in a cool place—55°F is ideal—until it ceases bubbling and the liquor clears. When the balloon goes limp, the wine is done fermenting. Bottle, cap tightly, and store in a cool, dark place. It should not be served for at least a month, and longer is better. However, this mead, unlike many other drinks, does not improve with really long aging, so it should be consumed within a year of the time it was made.

MAY DAY WINE

Serves 6 to 8

6 CUPS WHITE WINE

1/4 CUP SLICED FRESH
STRAWBERRIES

1/4 CUP SLICED FRESH
RASPBERRIES

12 SPRIGS WOODRUFF

1 ORANGE, THINLY SLICED,
FOR GARNISH

May Day is a fine time to drink this wine. Berries are beginning to come into season, and flowers are blooming everywhere. We dance around the maypole, often wearing wreaths on our heads made from woodruff, like the herb in this delicious wine. Faeries are frolicking about, making mischief or taking care to watch over their human friends. In accordance with the Beltane tradition of gathering flowers in a basket and placing a bouquet at the front door of their closest neighbors, why not add a bottle of this wine to your gift? Alternatively, invite friends and family over for a Beltane celebration. As you gather together, the wine will contribute to a feeling of community, spreading the lightness and merriment of the season. A toast for this wine goes like this:

May we always be held tight
In the circle of love as we are today.
If not in flesh, then always in spirit!

Pour the wine into a carafe or widemouthed bottle. Add the strawberries, raspberries, and woodruff. The berries add a sweet flavor, and the woodruff adds a smoothness. Allow the mixture to blend for at least 1 hour. Strain and serve well chilled. Garnish with orange slices.

Beltane Wine Punch

Serves 4 to 6

6 SPRIGS WOODRUFF

6 CUPS DRY WHITE WINE

1/2 CUP GRANULATED SUGAR

1/2 CUP WATER

1/2 CUP BRANDY

2 CUPS CHAMPAGNE, CHILLED

All through the night of April 30, ancient—as well as modern—pagans burn balefires or bonfires. As dawn breaks on May Day, they dance around the fire's embers. But before long, they stop dancing and quickly gather "May Dew" and rub it on their skin. It is believed that once every human eye has turned astray, the faeries sprinkle magical nectar on the dew that keeps one's complexion fresh. In the Land of Faery, time moves differently than the time we know and experience. Faeryland inhabitants retain their youthful appearance much longer than we do here on earth. This magical nectar is a special gift the faeries bestow on their human friends.

You, too, can participate in this age-old tradition. Before the dew evaporates on May 1, rush to gather the sweet moistness from the most delicate flowers, leaves, or blades of grass you can find (or whatever aspect of Mother Nature calls to you). If possible, leave the sprigs of woodruff outdoors overnight and use the dew that has gathered on them.

Begin by massaging the dew onto the area of your face you want the most assistance with. Thank Mother Nature and your faery friends for offering such a wonderful gift. Later, when you drink the wine, remember to toast to nature's devas.

Marinate the woodruff in the white wine for at least 1 hour. In a small saucepan, combine the sugar and water to make a syrup. Bring to a boil and stir until sugar melts, about 2 minutes.

Remove the woodruff from the white wine, and add brandy, sugar syrup, and champagne. Adjust the sweetness as desired.

SUMMER SOLSTICE

Summer Solstice (also known as Midsummer, Alban Hefin, and Litha) is celebrated on the first day of summer.

Summer Solstice is the longest day of the year, when the sun is at its zenith. The altar is decorated with roses and other summer flowers. If you have an herb garden, harvest herbs on this day. Herbs have reached full maturity and have the strongest potency at this time. A common practice among Wiccans that you can participate in is to banish all sorrows by placing your woes into a small bag of vervain or lavender. Other traditions that you can do to celebrate this sabbat include drying herbs, blueprinting leaves, leaving out food for the faeries who prevail throughout this season, searching for a walking stick, and weaving a God's Eye. It is also suggested that you light a red candle, as healing and love magic charms work best now.

Herbs and flowers associated with Summer Solstice include acorn, carnation, chamomile, cinquefoil, daisy, elder, fennel, hemp, ivy, larkspur, lavender, lily, male fern, mugwort, oak, pine, rose, Saint John's wort, wild thyme, wisteria, verbena, and yarrow.

Traditional foods for the Summer Solstice include yellow squash, zucchini, summer fruit, yellow and orange foods (as they are sun colors), pumpernickel bread, ice cream, ale, and mead.

Litha Avocado Salad

Serves 2

2 AVOCADOS, PITTED AND SKINNED

1/2 CUP BLUE CHEESE, CRUMBLED

1/2 CUP GORGONZOLA CHEESE, CRUMBLED

1/4 CUP RED ONION, SLICED VERY THIN

BALSAMIC VINEGAR

FRESHLY GROUND BLACK PEPPER

Second only to the olive, the avocado has the highest monounsaturated fatty acid content of any fruit. At 20 percent, this is almost twenty times that of any other fruit. Some people avoid avocados because they're afraid to consume the fat, but the monounsaturated fats actually help basal metabolic rate, reduce overeating, and assist the body in absorption of soluble vitamins like Vitamin E and other nutrients. Avocados also provide fiber, essential minerals like iron, copper, phosphorus and magnesium, as well as vitamins including A, several B-complex, especially B3 (folic acid), and a number of powerful antioxidants including vitamins C and E, calcium, iron, and potassium. In fact, the potassium content of an avocado is three times that of a banana. Avocados can help lower your cholesterol level and boost your immune system. So it time to ignore its undeserved reputation as a high-fat, high-calorie diet-buster, and embrace the avocado for the superfood that it is.

Litha is a time to celebrate the abundance in the fields and the constant turning of the Wheel of Life. Acknowledge that now is the time to shine brightly and boldly before making peace with the waning season and welcoming the contemplative darkness that is coming.

Slice the avocados into small chunks and plate. Cover with the cheeses, then the onions. Drizzle with balsamic vinegar and sprinkle with freshly ground black pepper.

Cucumber Salsa

3¹/₂ to 4 cups

6 CUCUMBERS, PEELED AND
CHOPPED

¹/₂ CUP CHOPPED JALAPEÑOS

¹/₄ CUP MINCED CILANTRO

3 TABLESPOONS FRESHLY
SQUEEZED LEMON JUICE

SALT AND PEPPER

he inherent properties of the cool cucumber mingled with the zesty salsa suggest the benefit that can arise from balancing opposites. Steady composure combined with passion and fire offer variety, adventure, and wholeness. Finding the right mix is like the swinging of a pendulum. To help you equalize the polarities of your opposite characteristics, look in a mirror or reflective water. Say

Mother/Father, Divine Source,
Allow me to always see the significance
Of blending the cool and calming influence
Along with the spicy, passionate side of my nature.
This will enable me to have a life balanced, whole, and creative.

This recipe comes from our sister Page Kistner, who has been interested in women's spirituality for several years.

Combine the cucumbers, jalapeños, and cilantro in a bowl. Sprinkle in the lemon juice, mixing well. Season with salt and pepper.

This salsa tastes delicious over fish, pork, beef, chicken, or salad. Alternatively, you can use it as a dip.

Lilith's Lily Fair Soup

Serves 4

1 MANGO, PEELED AND DICED

1 SMALL HONEYDEW MELON, RIND AND SEEDS REMOVED, CUT INTO 1-INCH CUBES

1/4 CUP FRESHLY SQUEEZED ORANGE JUICE

1 CUP SLICED FRESH RASPBERRIES

1 TABLESPOON GRANULATED SUGAR

2 TABLESPOONS GRAND MARNIER

5 ORGANIC DAYLILIES, RINSED AND GENTLY PATTED DRY

This soup was named after Lilith, Adam's first wife, because it combines the lushness of nature's fruits with the bold hint of liqueur. Both of these attributes were part of Lilith's own personality. She was thrown out of the Garden of Eden for being too outspoken and independent. Many people wrongly remember her as a sinful woman, when really her only crime was having a mind of her own. Today she is honored by Wiccans as a powerful free-speaking woman. Let us remember to speak our truth and have the integrity and wisdom to saturate our words with kindness and diplomacy to be understood and respected

Mangos are excellent for helping throw off distasteful body odors and are also a great blood cleanser with fever-soothing qualities. This soup is an excellent source of vitamin C, with the inclusion of raspberries, orange juice, and honeydew.

In increments, purée the mango, honeydew, and orange juice in a blender or food processor until smooth. Transfer to a bowl. Rinse the blender clean and purée the raspberries, sugar, and Grand Marnier. Transfer to a bowl. Chill both mixtures separately for 2 hours before serving. Spoon or ladle the melon mixture into one side of shallow soup bowls. Spoon or ladle the puréed raspberries on the other side, without mixing. Cut 1 daylily into thin strips. Sprinkle some strips into each bowl. Place 1 whole flower in each bowl. Serve immediately.

Midsummer Ale Bread

3 loaves

3 CUPS SELF-RISING FLOUR

2 TABLESPOONS
GRANULATED SUGAR

12 OUNCES ALE

1/2 CUP BUTTER, MELTED

The ancient custom of breaking bread is common to many cultures. There are infinite manifestations of this single act. In one interpretation, breaking bread symbolizes the sharing of oneself amongst loved ones gathered together under one roof.

Bake a fresh loaf of Midsummer Ale Bread for the next party you attend. With the breaking of the bread, dole out a piece to each guest. Invite them all to extend a prayer, a hope, or a wish for either the guest of honor, hosts, or whomever is the most needing of assistance. This ritual works well at a housewarming, retirement, birthday party, or wedding and baby showers. The warm energy that is the natural result of offering love will permeate every corner of every room throughout the house. As people consume the bread, they invite the Divine Spirit to work through them. Good feeling cycles through all present in the room.

Preheat the oven to 350°F. Mix the flour and sugar. Stir with a wooden spoon. In increments, blend in the ale. Transfer the batter into three 6 by 3-inch loaf pans, and drizzle the butter over the tops. Bake for 50 minutes.

Note: If you do not use self-rising flour, add 3 teaspoons baking powder and 1 1/2 teaspoons salt to the flour and sugar mixture.

Bejeweled Green Beans

Serves 4 to 6

1 CUP HARICOTS VERTS OR FRESH
GREEN BEANS

1/2 CUP OLIVE OIL

1/3 CUP WHITE VINEGAR

1/3 CUP DRY WHITE WINE

1 BAY LEAF, CRUMBLED

2 CLOVES GARLIC, MINCED

DASH OF HOT PEPPER SAUCE

1/2 TEASPOON MINCED
FRESH DILL

1/2 TEASPOON MINCED
FRESH THYME

SALT AND PEPPER

CHOPPED PARSLEY, FOR GARNISH

Green beans were introduced to Europe in the sixteenth century by early explorers who had traveled to South America. The most important nutritional value of green beans comes from their high level of protein.

Within the center of our physical being, protein prevails, keeping us strong. Within our spiritual being, trust prevails, providing the anchor on which all our relationships are built, especially the one that we hold with ourselves. When you are feeling unworthy and without a shred of confidence or trust in yourself and your abilities, try this pick-me-up technique. Look in the mirror, focusing on your right eye. Say

I love you, (your name here)
I forgive you for ever thinking you were bad, unworthy, or incapable.
You are innocent.
You are a beautiful child of the Universe.
All things are possible.
Success is your Divine right.

Rinse the beans and snap off the ends.

In a large saucepan, heat the oil. Add the beans, vinegar, wine, bay leaf, garlic, hot pepper sauce, dill, and thyme. Season with salt and pepper. Add just enough water to cover. Bring to a boil very slowly. Reduce the heat and simmer, covered, until the beans are crisp-tender, about 12 to 14 minutes (increase cooking time by 5 minutes for regular green beans). Remove from heat. Taste the liquid for seasoning and adjust.

To serve, drain the beans and sprinkle with chopped parsley. Leave the beans in the liquid if you need to refrigerate.

Note: Haricots verts are thin, delicate French green beans. If they aren't available, you can substitute any fresh green beans.

Noodles della Italia

Serves 4

16 OUNCES LINGUINE

1 CUP CHOPPED ONION

1 CUP CHOPPED RED BELL PEPPER

2 CLOVES GARLIC, MINCED

1/4 CUP SLICED FRESH BUTTON
MUSHROOMS

1 TABLESPOON CHOPPED
FRESH BASIL

1 TABLESPOON CHOPPED
FRESH OREGANO

2 TABLESPOONS OLIVE OIL

One religion that is similar to Wicca in many ways is Italian Witchcraft, also known as Stregheria, La Vecchia Religione, and simply the Ways. Streghe, witches of the Stregheria, utilize alchemy in their Witchcraft and spell casting, always adding elements and never removing any.

The Stregheria is a folkloric religion with roots that date back to the Latin and Etruscan cultures. It enjoyed a renewal in the fourteenth century when Aradia, the founder of the Triad Clans, received spiritual guidance that challenged the existing order. She taught the Ways by means of three traditions, known as the Fanarra, Janarra, and Tanarra. Fanarra protects the Earth Mysteries, Janarra focuses on the Lunar Mysteries, and Tanarra guards the Stellar Mysteries.

Her disciples and their descendants have kept the Ways alive for several generations, often through the clan spirits, known as the Lare. The Streghe believed that to keep their lore strong, the most faithful people must be born again to their descendants. The Lare protect the homes, but most important, they preserve family traditions. Succeeding generations help to remind us of all that is old and sacred. They bring us back to our roots, a place from which we can draw our true power and gifts.

This recipe comes to us from Tara's Aunt Norma Seefeldt.

Bring about 8 cups of water to a boil in a saucepan. Add the noodles and cook until al dente or to taste. Drain and set aside.

In a large skillet, sauté the onion, pepper, garlic, mushrooms, basil, and oregano in the olive oil. Remove the mixture from the skillet and mix it with the cooked noodles.

Vegetable Frittata

An athame, a ritualistic knife, is a common tool of many witches. Knives are an instrument of the element air, hence an athame can also be a sword, although any type of knife can be used. Traditionally, a knife with a white hilt is used for cooking and cutting purposes. When buying any item that will be used as a ritual tool, do not haggle over the price. Any task performed with a consecrated tool becomes sacred, thus cutting bread or vegetables for your family becomes a sacred act of love.

To call a knife an athame, you must first consecrate it with the four elements. Burn a purifying incense or oil, such as rosemary or sage, around the knife. Allow the smoke and fire to reach the blade of the knife. Sprinkle dirt from your own yard or a special plant over it. Rinse it clean with salt- or seawater. Wipe it dry and say a special prayer you want to infuse into your athame.

Alternatively, you may want to have two athames—one knife for culinary purposes and another reserved for your magical arts outside of food preparation. Athames are often engraved with symbols of love. Even today, when two people get married, the knife allocated for cutting the ceremonial wedding cake is engraved with the lovers' names and the wedding date. The athame is symbolic of the life force.

1 LARGE RED BELL PEPPER

1/2 TEASPOON FRESHLY GROUND
WHITE PEPPER

12 LARGE EGGS

1 CUP MILK

SMALL BUNCH OF SCALLIONS,
SLICED

1 TABLESPOON CHOPPED FRESH
BASIL PLUS 10 BASIL LEAVES,
FOR GARNISH

SALT AND PEPPER

5 OUNCES CRUMBLED FETA OR
GOAT CHEESE

1/2 TABLESPOON UNSALTED BUTTER

1/2 TABLESPOON OLIVE OIL

3 SMALL RED POTATOES,
THINLY SLICED

Roast the pepper either by holding it over a high gas flame or placing it under a broiler, turning the pepper until it is charcoal-black. Wrap the pepper in a paper towel, place it in a plastic bag, and let it sweat for 15 minutes. Rub off the skin with a paper towel. Slice the pepper into 1/4-inch-wide strips.

In a large bowl, combine the white pepper, eggs, milk, three-fourths of the scallions, basil, salt, pepper, and half the cheese. Set aside.

Heat the butter and oil in an ovenproof, preferably nonstick, 10-inch pan (see note) over medium heat. Add the potatoes, cooking on both sides until tender, about 10 minutes.

Preheat the oven to 350°F. Pour the egg mixture over the potatoes. Cook over medium heat. Pull back the edges with a spatula until the whole frittata is partially cooked, about 8 minutes.

Sprinkle the remaining cheese over the frittata. Place in the oven and cook until it is set in the middle, about 25 minutes.

Garnish with the basil. Serve immediately.

Elder Flower Chicken

Serves 4

2 POUNDS BONELESS
CHICKEN BREASTS

Sauce

3/4 CUP FRESH ELDER FLOWER
HEADS (5 TO 6 CLUSTERS)

SALT

4 EGG YOLKS

1/8 TEASPOON GROUND GINGER

ALMOND MILK (RECIPE OPPOSITE)

To find the freshest elder flower, harvest in June. The flowers will be whiter then and make a prettier sauce, although not necessarily a tastier ones. If possible, gather the flowers when they are in full bloom. Keep them until they are dry; then grind them and keep them for the whole year. Dried elder flowers are most easily found at health-food stores or whole-food markets.

Under the golden rays of the summer sun, an organic gardener picks the elder flower. In biodynamic gardening, it is believed that the sun's magnetic energy field draws the nutrients out of the roots. This brings the nutrients to the petals of the flower, where they reside all day until their return to the roots at night. This theory is evident by the insects drinking from its nectar, showing the gardener that the flower is ready for harvesting. In the Chinese philosophy, the vibrations of the elder flower are bitter and cool, which helps warm up the heart and lungs so we can be active in the heat of summer.

Place the chicken in a pot, with salted water to cover. Poach the chicken, simmering until cooked, approximately 35 minutes. Strain the broth and reserve 2 cups to make the almond milk. Set the chicken aside.

To make the sauce, carefully strip the elder flower heads from their green stems (try to get out all bits of green). Grind the elder flowers and salt to season in a mortar and pestle or food processor. Combine the flowers and almond milk in a saucepan. Beat the egg yolks and mix them into the almond milk mixture. Stir this sauce over fairly low heat until it thickens (avoid boiling). Season with ginger.

Skin the chicken pieces, and cover them with the sauce to serve.

You may substitute 2 to 3 egg yolks, plus 1 teaspoon rice, instead of the 4 egg yolks.

Note: While exact measurements may vary for different recipes, the ratio is always 3 parts almonds to 4 parts water or broth.

Almond Milk

About 3 cups

2 CUPS WATER OR
VEGETABLE BROTH

1 1/3 CUPS GROUND ALMONDS

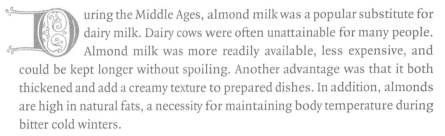During the Middle Ages, almond milk was a popular substitute for dairy milk. Dairy cows were often unattainable for many people. Almond milk was more readily available, less expensive, and could be kept longer without spoiling. Another advantage was that it both thickened and add a creamy texture to prepared dishes. In addition, almonds are high in natural fats, a necessity for maintaining body temperature during bitter cold winters.

Bring the water to a mild boil. Turn off the heat. Add the almonds, let steep for 10 minutes.

Cover a widemouthed pitcher with cheesecloth. Carefully pour half the almond mixture over the cloth, straining the milk and catching the almonds. When all the liquid has been strained, cautiously pour the remaining mixture over the cloth. Make sure the almond milk is not gritty. The thicker and smoother the milk, the better. If your milk comes out lumpy, we recommend you strain the mixture again. Alternatively, you may choose to force the mixture through a fine-mesh strainer or sieve. Save the strained almonds for use in other recipes.

Sun King Pork

People in the Middle Ages worshiped the life-giving sun as a god, especially during Midsummer, its peak of life. One ritual that glorifies the sun is the weaving of a God's Eye. Even today, children make God's Eyes, but they are not told their spiritual and historical significance. With an unobtrusive approach, this can be a great way to introduce children to the ideology of honoring nature and showing respect to the forces that enable us to survive.

You will need two sticks or dowels, a collection of colored yarn, glue, and scissors. Cut the dowels or sticks approximately 8 inches long. (Popsicle sticks work great, too!) Place them so they form an equilateral cross and glue them together at the center. Cut the yarn into lengths approximately 2 feet long. When the glue has dried, place a piece of yarn closer to the center on the right side of the horizontal stick, with the tail hanging away from you. Wind the yarn once up over the top of this stick. Move clockwise with the yarn going under the bottom stick. Again, weave the yarn up over the stick. Continue wrapping, periodically stopping to push the yarn toward the center so that you have a tight weave. When you are ready to introduce a new color, cut the first yarn, leaving a 1-inch tail. Tie the new string to the first yarn. Snip off the excess. Begin weaving again, working your design outward. The opposite side of what you will see will be the face of your God's Eye, so do not worry too much about how the side you are working on appears. You can work your yarn to the end of the sticks, or stop short. Either way, you may want to create a loop at the end of one stick to hang your creation.

We should remember how the sun has helped us all or given us glorious warm memories. As you gather together to weave a God's Eye, invite each of your guests to reflect on the glory of the sun and how it benefits them in particular. For younger children, you may want to suggest that this "eye" is one that will protect and watch over them. Alternatively, remind them of how we are warmed by the sunshine's golden rays and how all the food we eat is first nurtured by the sunshine.

3¹/₂ POUNDS LEAN PORK
SHOULDER OR BUTT

4 CLOVES GARLIC, THINLY SLICED

1¹/₄ CUPS FRESHLY SQUEEZED
ORANGE JUICE

¹/₄ CUP FRESHLY SQUEEZED
LIME JUICE

1 TABLESPOON GRATED
ORANGE PEEL

2 TEASPOONS GROUND CUMIN

1 TEASPOON MINCED FRESH
OREGANO LEAVES

1¹/₂ TABLESPOONS CORNSTARCH

1 TABLESPOON WATER

³/₄ CUP CHICKEN BROTH

¹/₄ CUP DRY WHITE WINE

SALT AND PEPPER

Bone, trim the fat off, and tie the pork. Without cutting the string, make small slashes all over the meat. Tuck the garlic slices into the slashes. In a large bowl, combine the orange juice, lime juice, orange peel, cumin, and oregano. Place the pork in the bowl, turning to coat all sides. Cover and refrigerate for at least 30 minutes and up to all day, turning the meat occasionally.

In a barbecue with a lid, mound and ignite sixty charcoal briquettes on the fire grate. When the coals are covered with ash, in 20 to 30 minutes, push half to each side of the fire grate. To maintain the heat, add five briquettes to each side now and every 30 minutes of cooking. Place a drip pan between the mounds of coal. Set the grill in place. Alternatively, you can turn a gas barbecue on high heat and heat, covered, for 10 minutes, then adjust for indirect, medium heat; set a drip pan beneath the grill.

Place the pork on the grill over the drip pan. Brush with a little of the marinade, then cover the grill, opening the vents. Reserve ¹/₂ cup of the marinade to brush over the meat occasionally as it cooks. Pour the remaining marinade into a 2- to 3-quart pan. Cook the pork until a thermometer inserted into the thickest part registers 165°F, at least 2¹/₄ hours. Brush the meat occasionally with the reserved marinade, salt and pepper to taste in the last 30 minutes of grilling. Transfer the roast to a platter and let stand in a warm place for at least 20 minutes (the interior will be pink, but it will turn white as the meat rests).

Mix the cornstarch with the water. Add the broth, wine, and cornstarch mixture to the pan with the marinade. Stir over high heat until the sauce is boiling.

Remove string from the pork and cut the meat into thin slices. Serve with the marinade gravy.

Sunshine Jell-O

Serves 6 to 8

1 (6-OUNCE) PACKAGE ORANGE
JELL-O

1 CUP HOT WATER

1 CUP COLD WATER

1 CUP FRESHLY SQUEEZED
ORANGE JUICE

1 CUP BUTTERMILK

1/4 CUP CHOPPED WALNUTS,
FOR GARNISH

1 (8-OUNCE) CAN MANDARIN
ORANGES, FOR GARNISH

Children are an integral part of the Wiccan community. They represent all that is exuberant and joyous about living. Invite children to participate in your ceremonies or rituals. They will provide a constant reminder to invite laughter and a light temperament to your ceremonies, especially if and when the unexpected happens, such as a candle that will not light or a mocking crow singing in the middle of a chant. Children are akin to angels and faeries, who fly because they live so joyously.

This favorite childhood dessert is included in *The Wicca Cookbook* to remind us of the importance of being silly and losing ourselves in laughter. Children know this lesson well and can be great teachers to the rest of us. As you prepare this dish, reminisce about your favorite childhood memory. Burn incense, bring in fragrant flowers, or play music that reminds you of when you were young. Relive the memory by sharing it or reenacting it when possible, especially in the company of children. Try to laugh at yourself and delight in the joy that is living.

Mix the Jell-O and hot water in a bowl. Add the cup of cold water, orange juice, and buttermilk. Pour into an 8 by 5-inch pan. Place in the refrigerator. When this creamier Jell-O begins to congeal, sprinkle the chopped walnuts and place the mandarin oranges on top.

This recipe was a favorite treat of Jamie's grandfather, Joe Martinez, a sweet man who could play a mean harmonica, made you feel like Ginger Rogers on the dance floor, and always let you know how much he loved you.

Midsummer Witches' Rose Dessert

Serves 4

1 CUP FRAGRANT ROSE PETALS,
WHITE BASES REMOVED

1 CUP MASHED BANANAS

1/2 CUP CHOPPED CURRANTS

2 TABLESPOONS MINCEMEAT

1/4 CUP WILD ROSE FAERY JAM
(PAGE 79)

1/2 CUP FRESHLY SQUEEZED
ORANGE JUICE

WHIPPED CREAM, FOR GARNISH

ROSE PETALS, FOR GARNISH

Midsummer is the time to enjoy summer flowers. Their majestic beauty takes us by surprise each season. Ancient people knew the Summer Solstice was the best time to harvest flowers, with the petals having the strongest potency at this time. Pick roses just as the flower opens completely.

It is imperative that prior to picking any plant, you acknowledge the living spirit who dwells within and ask permission to take any part of it. Mother Nature planted roses to demonstrate the power and strength of beauty. We should remember to honor Her gift and treat it with respect. When you first ask permission to pick a flower, you will find the plant's deva will direct you to the blossom, leaf, or stem it wants you to use. After you have asked permission to take flowers for this recipe, grasp the flower by the stem and pull off the petals all at once. If they are dirty, rinse them lightly under running water and dry them on paper towels. Handle them very gently so they don't bruise. This light dessert is the perfect treat for the Midsummer sabbat.

Place one layer of rose petals on a wide decorative dish. In a small bowl, mix the bananas, currants, and mincemeat. With the back of a spoon or spatula, spread a layer of the banana mixture over the petals. Leave some petals protruding around the edges. Cover with a layer of rose jam.

When ready to serve, pour the orange juice over the dessert. Top off with a layer of whipped cream. Garnish with rose petals.

Cherry Pottage

This dessert was a favorite medieval genteel dish, so it merited the rare use of cherished white sugar. Often we set aside those items we deem too precious for everyday use. Yet the china, Grandma's diamond earrings, and the priceless crystal excavated from the deepest mine are all symbols of prosperity. It is as if we are telling the Universe we can't handle prosperity because we don't know how to appreciate it or relish the joy it offers. Money and prosperity are fluid energy, and are not to be held too closely. Hoarding money can keep it from coming to you when you need it most.

Mother Nature works in a constant ebb and flow: perpetual motion. If something is withheld, the passage into the next cycle is blocked. When you pay for something, a bill or movie ticket, you extend a form of energy in expectation that you will receive something back. By infusing love and blessings into this give-and-take, we can hope to receive more prosperity. Write "thank you" in the memo section of your checks, especially as you send out your bills to show you appreciate the service already given or the one you hope to receive. The more goodness we cast forth, the more we will obtain.

Reflect on all that you have. To feel more affluent, take some time to recognize all the different kinds of prosperity you are enjoying, such as love of family and friends, work you enjoy, or a spirituality that makes you feel united to a greater love. Light a green candle to draw the prosperity to you and your home. Place a citrine gemstone, also known as the "merchant stone," in the palm of your hand. Say

> I attract to me,
> Money and prosperity.
> As is my Divine right,
> Abundance is in sight.
> I receive all willingly,
> And take most graciously.
> In all forms that appear,
> For it is goodness that I mirror.

Serves 6

1 QUART FRESH, RIPE
RED CHERRIES

1 1/2 CUPS RED WINE

2/3 CUP GRANULATED SUGAR

4 TABLESPOONS UNSALTED BUTTER

1 CUP SOFT BREAD CRUMBS

DASH OF SALT

FLOWERS, FOR GARNISH

COARSE SUGAR, FOR GARNISH

Wash the cherries and discard the stems and pits. Place the cherries, 2/3 cup of the wine, and half of the sugar in a blender and purée. Add a little more wine if you like. Melt the butter in a saucepan, over low heat. Add the fruit purée, bread crumbs, the remaining wine and sugar, and the salt. Simmer, stirring steadily, until the purée is very thick. Pour into a serving bowl and cover. Refrigerate to cool.

When quite cold, decorate the edge of the bowl with flowers and sprinkle coarse sugar over the center. Serve in individual bowls.

FRUITED ICED TEA

Serves 10

4 TEA BAGS

1 SCANT CUP GRANULATED SUGAR

4 CUPS BOILING WATER

1 CUP FRESHLY SQUEEZED
ORANGE JUICE

1 CUP PINEAPPLE JUICE

1 CUP FRESHLY SQUEEZED
LEMON JUICE

10 TO 12 MINT SPRIGS,
FOR GARNISH

10 TO 12 ORANGE SLICES,
FOR GARNISH

The tradition of June weddings was passed down to our modern society from ancient pagans. May marked the month of the sacred wedding ceremony between the Goddess and the God. Human marriages were postponed to follow behind the Divine, loving bond of the Goddess and God.

Many brides are nervous on their wedding day. Their throats are parched, their stomachs churning, and their nerves shot. If you find yourself honored to be "backstage" with a June bride, offer her a glass of Fruited Iced Tea served in a pretty cup. Remind her that the liquid, made from Mother Earth's fruit, is akin to the Goddess within each of us. Suggest that she is yet another manifestation of the Goddess, preparing to marry a facet of the God. Invite her to feel the strength of the Mother coursing through her as it once flowed through the fruit tree.

Present her with a single red rose and recite this traditional poem to help calm her fears:

> *Marry in the month of May*
> *Most surely you will rue the day.*
> *Marry in June when roses grow,*
> *And happiness you will always know.*

Make the tea with tea bags in boiling water. Transfer the tea to a large punch bowl or pitcher. Add the sugar and remaining liquids.

Garnish with mint sprigs and orange slices.

Summer Sangria

Serves 12

8 CUPS DRY WHITE WINE

1 CUP APPLE JUICE

1/4 CUP FRESHLY SQUEEZED
LIME JUICE

1/3 CUP GRAND MARNIER

3 TABLESPOONS GRANULATED
SUGAR

1 CUP SLICED FRESH RASPBERRIES

1 CUP SLICED FRESH
STRAWBERRIES

2 ORANGES, THINLY SLICED,
FOR GARNISH

1 LEMON, THINLY SLICED,
FOR GARNISH

1 LIME, THINLY SLICED,
FOR GARNISH

At the next summer wedding you attend, clink your glass with a spoon or knife, which asks the newlywed couple to kiss. Pass around of the Summer Sangria and offer this toast to the bride and groom:

In the sweetness of this first kiss of married life,
Let all bitterness be diluted
And your lives together be as one.

One way of binding friends and family at a marriage ceremony is through the lighting of a unity candle. Gather everyone in a circle around three unlit white candles. Just as circles are a symbol of something that has no beginning and no ending, love is everlasting. Acknowledge and thank everyone present for the time and devotion given for being present and supporting the two lovers. Light the first candle. Have the bride say

Today we unite in physical awareness.
We are attracted to each other and celebrate our closeness,
Acknowledging our bodies that bring us together to form a blissful union.

Light the second candle. Have the groom say

Today we unite in mental awareness.
We complement each other and respect our differences,
Allowing each other to grow and respond to the world in our own unique way.

Light the third candle. Have the couple say

Today we unite in spiritual awareness.
We ask the Goddess to bless us and keep us on the path of love and light,
Accepting each other and using the Divine presence in our souls and hearts.

Mix the wine, apple juice, lime juice, Grand Marnier, sugar, raspberries, and strawberries in a large pitcher. Garnish with the orange, lemon, and lime slices. Add ice cubes and stir to chill.

Rose Hip Wine

About 1 gallon

6 CUPS ROSE HIPS

1 GALLON BOILING WATER

6 CUPS GRANULATED SUGAR

Rose hips, the fruit of the rose bush, are valued as an important source of vitamin C. Sailors often ate rose hips in place of citrus to ward off scurvy. The rose has been used to heal such ailments as sore throats, to relieve colic, as a cream for dry or inflamed skin, and as a tonic for the mind.

Even in the middle of summer, we have dark days, days when you cannot seem to shake the veil of being alone or afraid. Roses are a gentle reminder of the beauty of each day, the present, a gift. As you sip this wine, meditate on all the gifts life has given you. Even if you can only think of the simplest of items to be grateful for, that's a beginning. A blade of grass, a drop of dew, or a delicate rose petal are all gifts from the Mother. Here's a toast for this wine:

Work like you don't need the money,
Love like you've never been hurt, and
Dance like nobody's watching.

Wash the rose hips and cut them in half. Place them in a large heat-proof or ceramic bowl and pour in boiling water. Stir well with a wooden spoon. Cover the bowl and let stand for 2 weeks in a cool, dry, and dark place.

Strain the liquid into another bowl and stir in the sugar until it is dissolved. Cover the bowl and leave it for 5 days, stirring daily.

Pour the wine into a 1-gallon container, making sure to leave space at the top of the container for the fermenting process. Cover the bottleneck with a balloon. When the balloon goes limp, the wine is done fermenting, which will take approximately 6 months.

Cork loosely. Keep in a refrigerator for 2 weeks. Place a surgical or other sterile tube into the wine, stopping 1 inch above the sediment. Siphon off the wine into another gallon, leaving the sediment in the original bottle. Discard the sediment.

LAMMAS

Lammas (also known as Lughnasad, Festival of Lugh, August Eve, Festival of Breads, and the First Festival or Harvest) is celebrated on August 1 or 2.

On Lughnasad, the altar is decorated with barley, oats, grain, wheat, bread, or fruit. On this sabbat, Wiccans pay homage to the waning Sun King as we anxiously await the upcoming harvest. Also known as the Festival of Bread, various kinds of bread are made, then shaped into forms, especially the sun or man, which is representative of the God. Lammas is an Anglo-Saxon word meaning "loaf-mass." All forms of corn, especially cornmeal, are also a mainstay of this sabbat. Providing nourishment in a variety of foods that cross cultural lines, corn is a comfort food for people of many nations. Now is the season to perform rituals of protection and hope, as the reward of a season of hard work is still unknown. Other traditions that you can do to celebrate this sabbat include weaving corn dollies and visiting orchards, lakes, fields, and wells.

Plants associated with Lughnasad include all grains, aloe, cornstalks, cyclamen, fenugreek, frankincense, heather, hollyhock, myrtle, sunflower, oak leaves, and wheat.

Traditional foods of Lughnasad include barley cakes, star-shaped cake or cookies, wild berries, apples, rice, bread (such as wheat, oat, and especially corn), nuts, roasted lamb, grapes, pears, potatoes, turnips, berry pies, elderberry wine, ale, and meadowsweet tea. Since we are celebrating the wheat and grain harvest, little meat is consumed at this sabbat.

Potato–Corn Chowder

Serves 12 to 14

1 CUP HALF-AND-HALF OR HEAVY
WHIPPING CREAM

2 CUPS PEELED AND DICED
POTATOES

1 (8-OUNCE) CAN CREAMED CORN

4 TABLESPOONS BUTTER

1 CUP MINCED ONION

1/2 CUP DICED CELERY

2 CLOVES GARLIC

3 CUPS MILK

4 CUPS VEGETABLE BROTH

1 (8-OUNCE) CAN CORN

1/2 TEASPOON WHITE PEPPER

1 TEASPOON SEA SALT

2 TEASPOONS MINCED FRESH BASIL

2 TEASPOONS MINCED FRESH
PARSLEY

1 TEASPOON *EACH* MINCED FRESH
OREGANO, THYME, ROSEMARY

When serving this soup, begin by giving thanks to each of the four directions, for each direction offers a gift and ingredient for this delicious soup. From the north, we receive parsley and celery; the east, basil and oregano; the west, sea salt and thyme; the south, white pepper and rosemary. Say

Thank you Goddess Gaia, Mother Earth,
For the bounty and the abundance.
Thank you to the life-giving Sun God,
For the energy that enables our food to grow.
Thank you to all for the gifts, lessons, and growth,
That comes to us from the circle of our lives.

Since we are on the brink of the harvest season, cream, milk, and butter are included in this dish to please the faery beings, who are very active during the harvest seasons and can help caretake our plantings.

Jeanette Reynolds, who has been involved with nature spirituality and faery folk all her life, contributed this recipe and ceremonial ritual. She has a deep appreciation and reverence for all life forms and believes the faery beings are a part of our lives.

Combine the cream, half of the diced potatoes, and the creamed corn in a blender. Blend until smooth.

In a large soup pot, melt the butter over medium heat, being careful not to burn it. Add the onions, celery, and garlic. Sauté until soft. Add the remaining ingredients and the potato mixture. Bring to a boil. Decrease heat and simmer for 35 to 40 minutes.

Serve hot with a flavorful warm bread, such as Cornbread (page 116).

Note: If you would prefer not to use canned vegetables, substitute 2 cups of corn that is frozen or fresh off the cob.

BARLEY AND MUSHROOM SOUP

Serves 8

12 CUPS WATER

2 CUPS DRIED SHIITAKE
MUSHROOMS

1 1/2 TO 2 POUNDS FLANK STEAK

SALT AND PEPPER

1 CUP DRY PEARL BARLEY

4 SHALLOTS, SLICED

2 TABLESPOONS VEGETABLE OIL

2 TABLESPOONS BEEF STOCK

4 CUPS MILK

4 TABLESPOONS FRESHLY
SQUEEZED LEMON JUICE

The celebration of the first harvest brings forth the blessing of the seed taking life and coming to fruition. With faith and labor, we indeed reap what we sow. Gratitude is an excellent way of focusing on the positive and removing any negative thoughts. If we learn to practice unconditional gratitude, we bring freedom to our self-imposed prison of anger and regret. Perceived past wrongs and injustices are our prison bars, but unreserved gratitude melts these prison bars. Hatred can lock us in a tiny cell of self-pity, keeping out those who bring love and laughter into our lives. Gratitude releases us from this prison we created.

Being aware of our gifts to the Universe helps to perpetuate and keep alive our abundance. There are also our waiting gifts, which are qualities that are waiting to unfold. To appreciate the goodness we receive from the Mother, after partaking of the barley soup, gather everyone together in a sitting circle. Say

From the Universe, we are grateful for all gifts.
For all the gifts we receive,
We keep the circle of life in motion by giving back.

Pass around a pouch or box filled with rocks, each of which contains a word that symbolizes the waiting gift, such as faith, integrity, generosity, perseverance, fortitude, love, hope, wonder, kindness, desire, discernment, or compassion. Invite each person to randomly choose a rock. This will be the symbol for their waiting gift, the gift they will bring back to the world.

In a large heavy pot or skillet, combine the water, mushrooms, and steak. Season with salt and pepper. Bring to a boil; decrease heat and simmer for 45 minutes.

Rinse and drain the barley. In a saucepan, sauté the barley and shallots in oil until the barley is lightly toasted. Add the barley and shallots to the soup and stir in the stock base. Simmer for 45 minutes longer, until barley is tender. Adjust seasonings. Gradually add the milk and lemon juice. Bring to a boil. Remove and slice the steak.

Serve the soup piping hot in soup bowls with the steak on the side.

CORNBREAD

Serves 10

2 CUPS ALL-PURPOSE FLOUR

2 CUPS CORNMEAL

1 TABLESPOON BAKING POWDER

1 TEASPOON SALT

3 TABLESPOONS GRANULATED SUGAR

4 LARGE EGGS

2 CUPS BUTTERMILK

1/2 CUP CORN OIL

1 CUP CORN KERNELS

A Wiccan tradition you can partake in to celebrate the Festival of Breads involves the breaking of bread. This custom is a continuing rite that can become a part of your ritual awakening with the Sun God throughout the years.

At dawn, offer the one-quarter of a loaf that was saved and frozen from last year's celebration to the birds, squirrels, or rabbits in your area. Later in the day, make a new loaf of bread. Insert a candle in the center of this bread. Sprinkle cornmeal (which is sacred to the God) clockwise around the loaf. Begin by honoring the spirits from each of the four elements. With an athame or other ritual item, draw an imaginary circle as your boundary. Call forth the spirits that will safeguard and guide you through this rite. If you choose to do this with others, invite them to pray to their guides or angels for protection. Feel the energy rise and the warm glow of loving spirits around you, the guests, and the circle.

Once the circle has been cast, walk clockwise around the circle three times. On each turn, thank the Sun God for lending His energy so that we may all grow strong and healthy and bask in His glorious warmth, and for the grain, corn, and other products He nurtures and nourishes with His healing and sustaining heat. Break the bread, saving one-quarter for next year. Pass the three-quarter loaf around for the guests to eat and enjoy.

Preheat the oven to 350°F. In a small bowl, mix together the flour, cornmeal, baking powder, salt, and sugar. Beat the eggs in a large bowl. Whisk the buttermilk, oil, and kernels into the beaten eggs. Add the egg mixture to the dry ingredients, just until combined. Be careful not to overmix, which causes air bubbles.

Pour the mixture into a pie pan, an 11 by 8-inch baking dish, or two small well-buttered pie tins. Bake for 1 hour, or until knife inserted in bread comes out clean. Remove from pan and cool on a wire rack.

Note: You can substitute 1 cup yogurt and 1 cup of milk for the buttermilk.

Herbed Flatbread

Serves 6

1 (1/4-OUNCE) PACKAGE ACTIVE
DRY YEAST

1 1/2 CUPS WARM WATER

1 TEASPOON HONEY

DASH OF SALT

3 TABLESPOONS OLIVE OIL, PLUS
EXTRA FOR GARNISH

2 CUPS ALL-PURPOSE FLOUR

1 TEASPOON MINCED FRESH
OREGANO

1 TEASPOON MINCED FRESH BASIL

2 TO 3 CLOVES GARLIC, MINCED

1/4 CUP OIL-PACKED SUNDRIED
TOMATOES, SLICED

1/4 CUP SLICED GREEN
OR BLACK OLIVES

1/3 CUP CRUMBLED FETA
OR GOAT CHEESE

The staff of life, bread brings to us all the elements of nature. Bread combines gifts of the earth (flour), water, a purifying ingredient (salt), and through air, the yeast provides the catalyst to leaven the bread. Fire is used to bake the bread, thus intermingling all the ancient, basic elements of life into bread.

Bread is prevalent on Lammas and is served in plenty at the feast of this day. To ancient pagans, the beginning of August marked the commencement of the grain and wheat harvest. People were quite attuned to nature, so they chose this time to honor and revere bread as the product of grain.

This recipe comes from Elise Higley, who lives attuned to the Mother, enjoying the simple life.

Blend the yeast and 1/4 cup of the warm water. Let stand for 5 to 10 minutes, until foaming. Mix the remaining water, the honey, salt, and olive oil into the yeast water. Let sit for 5 minutes, until foaming.

Add the flour and knead. Roll the dough into a ball. Drizzle with olive oil. Cover with a cloth for 1 hour.

Preheat the oven to 475°F. Punch down the dough in the center. Knead for approximately 5 minutes. Spread and press the dough onto an oiled baking sheet. Sprinkle with the oregano, basil, garlic, tomatoes, olives, and cheese. Drizzle with olive oil. Bake for 20 minutes, until golden.

Cut into squares and serve piping hot.

Note: You can substitute 1 cup whole-wheat flour for 1 cup of the all-purpose flour.

If you prefer dry-packed sundried tomatoes, blanch them in 2 cups boiling water for 1 minute before you slice them.

Sun Bread

Enough for 1 "sun" and 8 to 10
"wheat stalks"

1/2 CUP SHELLED SUNFLOWER
SEEDS

6 CUPS ALL-PURPOSE FLOUR

1 (1/4-OUNCE) PACKAGE RAPID-RISE
DRY YEAST

1 TABLESPOON SALT

2 TABLESPOONS GRANULATED
SUGAR

2 TABLESPOONS VEGETABLE OIL

2 CUPS WARM WATER

Glaze

1 EGG YOLK

1 TEASPOON WATER

4 TO 6 DROPS YELLOW FOOD
COLORING

Shaping bread into various forms is an ancient custom that celebrates two of the main elements of this late summer holiday, wheat and the sun. Lammas reveres the Sun God, who shall be leaving us soon as we recede into the darkness and womb of the Goddess. With bread, we make the form of the God, the sun, and man in remembrance of basking in His glory for six months. We celebrate His warmth and honor His gifts to us by shaping bread harvested from His light.

Jeanne Morrow provided the guidance for shaping this bread. Jeanne grounds herself by creating with gifts from the earth, such as molding clay, gardening, and making bread.

Grind the sunflower seeds with a mortar and pestle. Mix with the flour. In a large bowl, combine the yeast, flour mixture, salt, sugar, and oil. Pour in the water, mixing well.

Turn the dough out onto a floured surface. Knead for 10 to 15 minutes. Return to the bowl. Cover with a cloth and let stand for 10 to 15 minutes. Cover a baking sheet with cornmeal.

Preheat the oven to 350°F. Turn the dough out onto a floured surface. Pat down to a circle, flattened to at least 1 inch thick and 10 to 12 inches wide. Cut 10 to 12 triangles around the perimeter of the circle. Set aside the excess dough. Arrange the rays to your liking. Transfer to a baking sheet. Use a portion of the excess dough to form the features of your sun's face (the nose, eyes, and mouth). With the remaining dough, roll out 8 to 10 thin breadsticks. With kitchen scissors, snip small slashes at one end. The result will be a resemblance to wheat stalks. Place the breadsticks 1 inch apart on a greased baking sheet.

Bake the sun and breadsticks for 15 minutes. In a small bowl, combine the egg yolk, water, and yellow food coloring. Paint the sun face with the food coloring mixture. You may choose to combine different coloring with the parts of the yolk and water mixture to accent the facial features or paint the rays.

Return the sun to the oven, along with the breadsticks. Continue to bake for another 12 to 15 minutes.

Lugh's Corn Casserole

uring this season, Lugh (pronounced loo), the Celtic Sun God, is honored for all that he offers us during this season. With this first harvest of wheat and grain also comes the reaping of corn. Corn is sacred to both pagans and Native Americans; both of whom use stones in ritualistic work.

Native Americans use the "stone people" to help them connect with Mother Earth. Although methods of sweat lodge ceremonies vary from tribe to tribe, one sweat lodge that I, Jamie, attended was set up as follows: a fire was built outside the tent, with stones thrown in it to get red hot. On cue, the keeper of the stones reached outside the closed tent flap and, with two small sturdy branches, collected the red-hot stones. He carefully placed the stones in a hole that was dug in the center. The leader sprinkled consecrated water on the stones, asking for guidance. The steam and heat rose, bringing an altered state of consciousness to the people inside. Messages were sent to and received from the stone people. We chanted, drummed, and sang. Some two hours later we emerged and lay on the moist earth, breathing in time with the Great Mother; we were cleansed. Each ceremony is sacred and different and quite often so intimate that they are never repeated in the same way.

Celtic pagans have long looked on Stonehenge and Avebury in England as locations for divining the future, giving them a sense of solidity, strength, and the power of the mystics. According to Celtic mythology, Lugh also attuned himself with the stone people. Lugh's father was stoned to death and then buried six feet deep under the very same stones, which called to Lugh and guided him to his father. When he came to accuse his father's killers, he emerged from the East, just as the sun appears to us every morning. His golden rays of righteous radiance splintered across the countryside to bring the truth to light.

Continues on next page

Serves 8

4 CUPS CANNED OR FROZEN CORN

4 EGG YOLKS

2 TABLESPOONS GRANULATED
SUGAR

SALT AND PEPPER

1 TABLESPOONS OLIVE OIL

1 TABLESPOON BUTTER

1 LARGE YELLOW ONION, CHOPPED

1 CLOVE GARLIC, SLICED

1 GREEN BELL PEPPER, CHOPPED

2 SERRANO CHILES, SEEDED
AND MINCED

4 OUNCES EXTRA-FIRM TOFU

1 (16-OUNCE) CAN STEWED
TOMATOES, DICED

2 TEASPOONS MINCED FRESH
OREGANO

Stones, gems, and crystals are the keepers of historical record for Mother Earth. They possess the secrets that we learn from or fail by. You may want to collect all your precious stone familiars. Sit quietly with them. The stones work as catalysts to help you find the answers within your own heart. Gemstones possess unique properties that can assist you in a variety of problems and situations. Use the stones wisely, and know that you were born with all the knowledge of the Universe: you just need to remember.

Jennifer DeVeoux donated this recipe.

In a food processor or blender, mix together the corn, egg yolks, and sugar, until well blended. Season with salt and pepper. Lightly butter a 2-quart casserole dish. Spoon in half the corn mixture. Set aside.

Heat the olive oil and butter in a large skillet, until the butter is melted. Sauté the onion for 3 minutes, until soft. Add the garlic, bell pepper, and chiles. Sauté until the pepper is soft. Add the tofu. Tomatoes, and oregano. Season again with salt and pepper. Let stew for approximately 20 minutes to combine the flavors.

Preheat the oven to 350°F. Spoon this filling over the corn mixture in the casserole dish. Spoon the rest of the corn mixture over the filling. Bake for 25 to 35 minutes until golden brown on top and bubbling.

Sun Rice

Serves 6 as a side dish

1 1/2 CUPS WATER

1 CUP UNCOOKED WHITE RICE

SALT AND PEPPER

4 TABLESPOONS BUTTER

PEEL OF 1/2 LEMON

JUICE OF 1/2 LEMON

3/4 CUP LIGHT WHIPPING CREAM, WARMED

CHOPPED FRESH PARSLEY, FOR GARNISH

The sun symbolizes the God and male energy. Both male and female energies are needed to make us complete, and as taught in Wiccan lore, the Goddess and the God represent these energies.

A harmonious life requires the equality of these two forces. This sabbat marks the beginning of the Goddess's six-month reign, therefore it is suggested you balance and center before inner work begins. Male energy emerges as the sun—thinking, seeing, and doing. Female energy appears as the moon—nurturing, feeling, and being still. When in balance, the polarity of the male and female energies complete and complement each other.

If you are experiencing uncomfortable swings in your mood or outlook on life, try this exercise to help achieve a more harmonious balance. Light a black or dark blue candle to symbolize the dark quietness of female energy. Light a white or yellow candle to represent the dynamic light of the male energy. Close your eyes and ask yourself the following questions. Take your time, sit still, and wait silently for an answer.

Where in my life do I find myself exerting too much energy, doing too much, even to the point of exhaustion?
Where in my life do I find myself deprived, diminished, or feeling without?
What can I do to bring greater balance to my life?

Calmly, yet with authority, take action concerning the answers given.

Bring the water to a rolling boil in a saucepan. Add the rice to the boiling water. Season with salt and pepper. Decrease heat. Simmer, covered, for 20 minutes, until rice is tender, stirring occasionally.

In a small skillet, melt the butter. Sauté the lemon peel for about 3 minutes. Remove the peel from the skillet. Add the butter to the cooked rice. Drizzle in the lemon juice, to taste. Gently fold in half the warmed cream. Add enough of the remaining cream to coat all the grains of rice.

Transfer to a serving dish. Garnish with chopped parsley.

Cú Chulainn Pasta

Mystical circumstances surround the origin of Sétanta, the greatest of Irish Celtic warriors. Dechtine, sister of Conchobar mac Nesssa, gave birth to him after mysteriously becoming pregnant by Lugh, the Irish god for which the holiday Lughnasah was named. From the moment he emerged from the womb, Sétanta could swim like a fish, and had seven fingers on each hand, seven toes on each foot, and seven pupils in each eye. Most troubling was the rage that came over him when he felt wronged and the transformation in his appearance: his bright orange hair stuck out wildly in every direction; his right eye would bulge hideously out of its socket; and his fourteen fingers would ball into fists, ready to fight all comers. At the age of seven, young Sétanta went to his uncle's court to train as a warrior. Upon his arrival, 150 boy warriors blocked his way, taunting and jeering. The lad flew into a tantrum and soundly beat all 150 youthful rivals into submission.

As he grew older, Sétanta often ran with wild abandon through the woods and fields of his uncle's kingdom, stirring up great winds as he sprinted across the landscape. Around the time that Sétanta neared manhood, his uncle Conchobar received an invitation to attend a great feast at the home of one of his subjects, Culann the smith. The king sought out his nephew to invite him along, but Sétanta was practicing hurling his spear while driving his chariot and ignored the request. The king went on his way, leaving the young man behind. When Sétanta finished his game and realized he was alone, he remembered his uncle's request. Believing that he had been abandoned, a great rage overtook over him. He followed the trail to Culann's dwelling, running fast as the wind pushes waves across the sea. As he drew near, he heard the sounds of celebration, but could not proceed. He was stopped by the ferocious Hound of Culann who guarded the home. Sétanta slew the beast, leaving the smith's lands unprotected. Culann and his guests lamented the loss of the great canine protector. Their grief awoke something within Sétanta, and he realized how his fit of temper had caused great harm. At that moment, he swore to be the defender of Culann's lands and all of

8 OUNCES SPAGHETTI OR
LINGUINE

3 CARROTS, PEELED

3 ZUCCHINI

3 CROOKNECK SQUASH

1 TABLESPOON OLIVE OIL

1 TABLESPOON BUTTER

2 CLOVES GARLIC, MINCED

1¹/₂ CUPS MINCED FRESH
BASIL LEAVES

³/₄ CUP MINCED FRESH PARSLEY

¹/₂ CUP MINCED FRESH CHIVES

2 TABLESPOONS MINCED FRESH
MARJORAM

DASH OF SALT

¹/₂ CUP GRATED PARMESAN CHEESE

Ulster. He became known as Cú Chulainn, the Hound of Culann. As the years passed, he became a favorite among the Celtic people, much like the Greek hero Achilles.

Cú Chulainn's tale is like the child who doesn't fit neatly into a box, who may be misunderstood or considered troublesome, but is, nevertheless, full of extraordinary talents. He might be socially awkward or ultrasensitive or full of pent-up frustration, but he may also be talented at sports or music or art. When given the right support and understanding, children like these grow up to become the heroes of their own lives.

David Westlake, storyteller extraordinaire, regaled us with the tale of Cú Chulainn.

Bring 4 cups of lightly salted water to a boil in a saucepan. Stir in the pasta and cook until al dente or to taste. Drain and set aside.

Cut the carrots, zucchini, and squash into long julienne strips, about ¹/₈ inch thick.

In a large skillet, warm the oil and butter over low heat. Add the garlic and carrots. Sauté for 5 minutes. Add the pasta, zucchini, squash, basil, parsley, chives, marjoram, and salt. Gently toss to combine. Cook for 5 minutes. Remove from heat and place in a serving bowl. Sprinkle with cheese and toss to combine. Serve immediately.

GRILLED TROUT

1 CUP ALL-PURPOSE FLOUR

1/2 TEASPOON CHOPPED FRESH
PARSLEY

1 TEASPOON MINCED FRESH
MARJORAM

6 TO 12 SMALL SPRIGS THYME,
SAGE, OR ROSEMARY

4 (12- TO 16-OUNCE) FRESH TROUT

1/2 TEASPOON COARSE SEA SALT,
OR TO TASTE

1/2 TEASPOON FRESHLY GROUND
PEPPER, OR TO TASTE

1/2 CUP BUTTER, MELTED

JUICE OF 1 LEMON

ater immersion is yet another ceremonial technique used to connect with the Mother. Since the trout comes from this blessed liquid source, purification by water is the perfect association with this dish. Purification is the process of clearing away the mundane as you prepare to enter the sacred.

Begin by thanking the fish for sacrificing its life so that you may partake of its energy and utilize it for food. As you wash and cleanse the fish, notice the water rinsing away all of the impurities. Even though every aspect of the Mother's world is already sacred, you must understand that this is so. It is your viewpoint that must see the sacredness of all things. Your attitude is everything. What you believe becomes what you see. Look around you with eyes of love. Look for the beauty in the mundane until life sparkles with the effervescent glow of love.

Position the rack 4 to 6 inches from the heat in a medium-hot grill. Combine the flour, parsley, and marjoram. Tuck 2 to 3 small sprigs of fresh herbs inside each trout. Dredge the trout in the flour mixture. Season with salt and pepper, and sprinkle each side with melted butter.

Place immediately on the grill rack. Grill for 8 to 10 minutes per inch of thickness (measured at the thickest part), turning once after 4 to 5 minutes. To test for doneness, place a fork in the thickest part of the fish. Gently twist the fork; when the fish flakes easily, it is ready. Drizzle the juice of a fresh lemon over the fish.

Raspberry Nutty Muffins

12 muffins

1¹/₂ CUPS ALL-PURPOSE FLOUR

¹/₂ TEASPOON BAKING SODA

¹/₂ TEASPOON SALT

1 TEASPOON GROUND CINNAMON

¹/₂ TEASPOON GRATED NUTMEG

1 CUP GRANULATED SUGAR

1³/₄ CUPS RASPBERRIES

2 LARGE EGGS, BEATEN WELL

¹/₂ CUP CHOPPED PECANS

²/₃ CUP VEGETABLE OIL

¹/₄ CUP UNSALTED SUNFLOWER
SEEDS, TOASTED

The young and the young at heart will enjoy these delicious muffins and the ancient custom of creating corn dollies or kirn babies for the Lammas celebration. Corn dollies are traditionally made from straw or cornhusks.

You need glue or a glue gun, several sheaves of straw, wheat, or cornhusks, and decorative items such as ribbons, yarn, buttons, beads, felt, fabric, toothpicks, confetti, or raffia. Soak the straw, wheat, or cornhusks for one hour. Wrap the straw over a ball of straw, wheat, or cornhusk, making sure to completely cover it. With a string or piece of ribbon, tie the straw together under the ball (at the neck). You can either tie the body, arms, or legs separately to the straws hanging down or leave the straw to dangle freely. You can attach ribbons, yarn, or raffia to the head for hair. If you choose, glue on (a glue gun works best) buttons, fabric, felt, or beads for the eyes, nose, and mouth. Glue confetti, ribbon, or fabric to the straw to decorate the clothing.

You may want to place your corn dollies or kirn babies on your Lammas altar to symbolize the first harvest and abundance of Mother Earth. It is also customary to bury or burn last year's dolly for good luck.

Preheat the oven to 400°F. Combine the flour, soda, salt, cinnamon, nutmeg, and sugar in a mixing bowl. Make a well in the center of the mixture. Place the berries and beaten eggs in the well, mixing well. Add the pecans and oil and mix thoroughly.

Spoon the batter into lightly greased muffin tins. Sprinkle the sunflower seeds over the muffins. Don't worry if the muffin tins are full; the batter is heavy, so it will not overflow.

Bake for 15 to 20 minutes. Cool for 5 minutes before removing from pan.

Berry, Honey, and Hazelnut Crumble

t their peak in the middle of summer, berries can be enjoyed with family and friends or in luxuriant solitude. After separating the berries from the leaves, set aside the leaves. To maintain the plant's vigor, never take more than one-third of the plant's leaves. Raspberry leaves can be made into a delicious tea to accompany dessert and is useful for a Wiccan Baby Blessing (recipe follows).

Raspberry leaves have long been a classic herbal recipe throughout China and Europe for pregnant women preparing for childbirth, as they help strengthen the uterus. Host a Baby Blessing for someone who is expecting a baby. At this ceremony, the pregnant woman is revered as a priceless jewel, because she is helping to cocreate life with the Mother.

Light a white candle for all the guests in the room, a pink candle for the expectant mother, and a red candle for the baby. The white candle symbolizes a bubble of pure protection; red, vitality and burgeoning life; and pink, unconditional love. As you light the candles chant

> Where there is love, there is no fear;
> Where there is no fear, there is no pain.

Allow the crescendo of the chant to become like a wave. Invite your guests to "ride the wave" with you, just as the pregnant mother will need to learn to ride each contraction, flowing with it rather than fighting against it. Each person can also present the guest of honor with a special gem, amulet, rock, or talisman, which will serve as a link that enables her to call on their strength during childbirth.

Serve the tea with this dessert. Present the expectant mother with any of the following: a special pouch for the talismans, a throne or special chair for the Blessing, the singing or chanting of songs of endurance or strength, and pampering, such as brushing her hair, massaging her feet or back, applying lotion to her arms, legs and feet, or painting her nails. All this will renew her energy and lend her strength. It is a blessing and an honor to be chosen to carry life. If the Mother has chosen to honor this woman, so should we.

Serves 8 to 10

5 CUPS MIXED FRESH SUMMER
BERRIES (BLACKBERRIES,
RASPBERRIES, STRAWBERRIES,
LOGANBERRIES, OR BLUEBERRIES)

HONEY OR LIGHT BROWN SUGAR

1/2 CUP HAZELNUTS, SKINNED
AND TOASTED

1/2 CUP WHOLE-WHEAT
BREAD CRUMBS

WHIPPED CREAM, FOR GARNISH

Raspberry Leaves Tea

WATER

2 TABLESPOONS FRESH
RASPBERRY LEAVES PER CUP
OF WATER PLUS 2 TABLESPOONS
FRESH RASPBERRY LEAVES

Preheat the oven to 350°F. Pour about 1 inch of water into a saucepan. Add the berries and cook gently over low heat for 10 to 15 minutes, until the fruits are soft without being mushy. Drizzle honey or sprinkle brown sugar over the top. Drain and reserve the excess juice.

Chop the hazelnuts as finely as possible. Mix the nuts with the bread crumbs. Ladle the berry mixture into a baking dish and cover the fruit with a thick layer of the bread crumb and nut mixture. Bake for 20 to 30 minutes, until the top is golden brown.

Warm the leftover juice. Drizzle the juice over the dessert. Top with whipped cream.

Bring the water to a rolling boil. Toss the raspberry leaves into a teapot, using the 2 extra tablespoons of leaves "for the teapot." Pour in the boiling water and let the tea steep for about 5 minutes (depending on how strong you like your tea). Strain the leaves out before serving the tea.

BLACKBERRY PUDDING

uring the Festival of Lugh, we not only include dishes that represent the products of the harvest (such as the rice flour of this dessert), but we also remember and honor Lugh, the Celtic god of light.

The myth of Lugh began in Ireland. The story goes that Balor, the Formorian king, was told that he would be slain by his own grandchild, so he locked up his only daughter, Ethlinn, in a high, secluded tower. One of Balor's enemies sneaked into the castle and became smitten with Ethlinn, who later gave birth to three sons who were summarily sentenced to death. But one child, Lugh, escaped his murderer and was raised in Balor's enemy territory of Danae.

A smith fostered Lugh, teaching him all his skill. In addition, it is believed Lugh dwelt within Faeryland. According to Irish belief, unless you possess the ability to pass between the two worlds, like Lugh, only human harpers who overhear the faerys' revelry are privy to their sweet melodies. Lugh came to be known as Samildanach, the Many Skilled. He was a poet, harper, smith, carpenter, scientist, physician, and more, mastering all artistic and medicinal fields.

Lugh carried with him a mighty sword named Fragarach, the Answerer, which helped him fight against injustice and all forms of slavery. Lugh fought his grandfather, Balor, in battle and killed him as predicted. Lugh is also called Lugh of the Long Hand or Long Arm. When he appeared to the Danaan chieftains, it is said that they felt as if they were watching the rising sun. The name is believed to be symbolic of the long stretching arms of the late summer sun's golden rays.

As you enjoy this summertime treat, reflect upon the great Sun God, who ripened the berries and helped make them so sweet. When you need his warmth and comfort, call on Lugh, and his sword of light will cut through your woes and bring you protection and love.

Serves 4 to 6

1¼ CUPS ALMOND MILK
(PAGE 101)

¼ TO ½ CUP GROUND ALMONDS

1¼ CUPS WATER

1 PINT FRESH BLACKBERRIES

⅓ CUP MERLOT OR OTHER
RED WINE

2 TABLESPOONS RICE FLOUR

⅓ TEASPOON GRANULATED SUGAR

½ TEASPOON SALT

⅛ TEASPOON GROUND GINGER

⅛ TEASPOON GROUND
CINNAMON

1 TABLESPOON BUTTER, AT ROOM
TEMPERATURE

2 TABLESPOONS RED WINE
VINEGAR

¼ CUP CURRANTS OR RAISINS

WHIPPED CREAM, FOR GARNISH

Combine the almond milk with the almonds and the water. Place the blackberries in a bowl and pour the wine over them, mixing gently. Some of the liquid will be soaked up by the berries. Pour off the remaining wine and discard. Use a blender or food processor to combine the berries with the rice flour, sugar, salt, spices, and almond milk until well blended. Pour the mixture into a large saucepan. Bring to a boil over medium heat, stirring constantly. Once a rolling boil has been achieved, let boil for about 2 minutes to thicken. Remove from heat and stir in first the butter, then the vinegar and currants.

Pour into a large serving bowl or individual dessert dishes. Chill for 20 to 30 minutes. Top with whipped cream.

Lammas Cooler

Serves 4

1/2 CUP BOYSENBERRY PURÉE
(RECIPE FOLLOWS)

1/2 CUP FRESHLY SQUEEZED
LIME JUICE

6 TABLESPOONS SUPERFINE SUGAR

3 CUPS MINERAL WATER, CHILLED

MINT SPRIGS, FOR GARNISH

Purée

2 CUPS FRESH BOYSENBERRIES

2 TABLESPOONS GRANULATED
SUGAR

During the glorious summer days, a depressed and lonely heart sometimes seems more pervasive. We often feel as if the warm sunshine should be able to lift our spirits, or that with so much of life buzzing around us, we should be able to shake the doldrums. But this is not always the case.

To cast a spell to drive away a despondent and melancholy mood, first cast a circle by drawing a circle in the air with your athame or index and middle finger pressed together. Walk clockwise in a circle, paying respect to and honoring each of the four directions. Thank Mother Earth and Father Sun for their gifts and know they are with you. Call in any other spirit guides to assist you in this rite. Ground yourself by sending your energy deep into Mother Earth. Feel the connection with you and all that is.

Light a blue candle. Direct all your loneliness, hurt, anger, and depression into the fire of the candle. Watch the flame grow. Listen for the still, small voice of the Mother. Hear the words you long to hear: "It is okay to be sad. This hurt will pass. I am with you." Feel the warm embrace of the Mother and the Father. Ground yourself with their Divine love by turning your palms upward to receive the warmth of the Sun God, sending your energy downward toward Mother Earth.

You will feel much lighter, and the wave of depression shall be lifted and taken away from you.

To make the purée, place the berries and sugar in a blender. Whirl until smooth, discarding the seeds.

In a small mixing bowl, stir the purée, lime juice, and sugar until the sugar is dissolved. Divide the mixture into highball glasses filled with ice. Stir in the mineral water and garnish with mint sprigs.

Rose Water

1 cup

Petals from 2 fresh roses

1 cup water

Roses are known to possess gentle healing powers and can be used for both culinary and healing purposes. You can spritz rose water around a room to refresh it. You may use it to induce a romantic occasion or saturate a washcloth with it and place it over your eyes to soothe a tired psyche. It can be used to cleanse the hands in ceremonial rituals. Alternatively, you can anoint the heads of ritual participants with rose water, which may encourage their stubborn egos to settle down and allow the rose's soft curative abilities to take effect. Try sprinkling it around your home: the smell will welcome friends, family, and the faery folk.

Rose water has also been used to forecast the future in love and romance. Just drizzle rose water on a yarrow sprig and place it under your pillow. If you awaken to find a wilted herb, there is no love in your future; if the yarrow is healthy, you can count on eternal blessing in your life.

Place the petals and water in a small saucepan. Warm slowly, until the petals turn translucent. Strain and use the liquid for cooking or spritzing.

Store in the refrigerator.

Luscious Lavender Lemonade

Serves 6

5 CUPS WATER

1/2 CUP LAVENDER FLOWERS, STEMMED

1/3 CUP FRESHLY SQUEEZED LEMON JUICE

1/2 CUP GRANULATED SUGAR

MINT LEAVES, FOR GARNISH

LAVENDER SPRIGS, FOR GARNISH

The fresh sweetness of this delectable drink will quench the strongest of thirsts brought on by the hot August sun during the Lammas celebration. The summer sun invites us to quench our thirst with this turn of the wheel as we begin our first harvest. If you grew your own lavender or are picking it fresh, try to maintain a sense of hope and wonder as you harvest the lavender blooms for this drink. Now is the time to recognize all the goodness we have reaped throughout the year.

The lavender has its own gifts to offer us. Lavender's healing properties include balancing energy and emotion, soothing the mind, enhancing intuition, clearing negative energy, promoting clarity, and normalizing mood swings. Still today, children in rural France are given lavender baths to keep them healthy and calm. Lavender's heavenly scent drew many ancient people to its purple dress. It inspired the French herbalist Maurice Mességué to acclaim this about the precious lavender: "It is one wonder and joy of the south on its blue dress, and its scent is God's gift to Earth. No scent could be sweeter."

In a small saucepan, bring 1 cup of the water to a rolling boil. Remove from heat and add the lavender blooms. Cover and steep for 10 minutes. Strain the mixture through a fine-mesh sieve; discard the lavender blossoms and set the tea aside.

Add the lemon juice and sugar to the remaining water. Add the prepared lavender tea. Refrigerate until chilled.

Garnish with mint leaves and lavender sprigs.

AUTUMNAL EQUINOX

Autumnal Equinox (also known as the Fall Sabbat, Alban Elfed, Mabon, Harvest Home, and the Second Festival of Harvest) is celebrated on the first day of fall.

The Autumnal Equinox marks the commencement of the thanksgiving and joy as the second harvest begins. Altars are decorated with acorns, wheat stalks, oat sprigs, pine- and cypress cones, vines, garlands of greenery and apples, and other fall fruits, flowers, and grain. This is the time for meditation and introspection. As the days become shorter and darker, the Autumnal Equinox offers us the opportunity to explore those faces of our being that we seldom honor, much less acknowledge. Like the rest of nature, we are moving into the darkness before creation. In soul and spirit, we are invited to travel down to our roots for nurturing, where we can gather strength and energy for yet another season of growing. But just as black contains all the colors of the rainbow, the darkness grants us a window into all aspects of our nature. We can make friends with our shadow selves, discover answers to questions only we can unravel, or just sit quietly in the stillness. Visiting the unknown can be a scary path, but it is only through the night that we reach the brilliance of another day. The journey is well worth the effort.

The Autumnal Equinox celebrates the sun child known as Mabon, a Welsh god who symbolizes the essence of the male aspect needed for fertility. We pursue the sacred stag as a representation of seeking that spirit of male energy. Once garnered, that male essence, the very spirit of the field, will be used for future crops. The theory is akin to saving seeds from plants and annual flowers and planting those seeds the next year. The idea is that by building on thriving vegetation, the subsequent harvests will be stronger and even more abundant.

Some believe Mabon is the counterpart to Persephone, daughter of Demeter, the goddess of all growing things, especially because both Mabon and Persephone were separated from their mothers and lived in a world without light. According to legend, the ground opened, forming a huge chasm when Persephone plucked a solitary flower. The girl ventured into the dark Underworld until she came upon Hades, lord of this dismal place. He offered her a handful of pomegranate seeds, from which she ate six ruby-red seeds. Because she ate food from the Underworld, she had to live there for one month per seed. Demeter mourned her daughter so intensely that during her absence she would not allow anything to grow; this marks our scarce seasons of fall and winter. Together, both Mabon and Persephone provide the bridge between the living and the dead. They remind the living that there is death so they will live a full life, and they show the dead the way to rebirth.

Traditions that celebrate this sabbat include making horns of plenty and rattles, placing multicolored leaves in baskets, taking meditative walks, gathering seedpods and dried plants, and quilting.

Herbs and flowers associated with the Autumnal Equinox include acorn, aster, aspen, benzoin, cypress, fern, hazel, honeysuckle, marigold, milkweed, chrysanthemum, myrrh, oak leaves, passionflower, pine, rose, sage, Solomon's seal, thistle, and wheat stalks.

Traditional foods of the Autumnal Equinox include underground vegetables (such as carrots, onions, and potatoes), corn and wheat products, bread, nuts, apples, cider, harvest gleanings, cornbread, beans, baked squash, and pomegranates.

Dionysian Stuffed Grape Leaves— Food of the Gods

The ancient Greeks had an incredible pantheon. Their gods and goddesses personified both their nature-based beliefs and their interpretations of cosmic forces. Dionysus was most commonly associated with wine and grapes. To his priestesses, the Maeriads (also called Maenads), wine was their sacrament. Along with the flesh of ritually slain game, such as deer, Dionysus, the prototype for Christ, represented the Divine sacrifice whose symbolic death would ensure the life and fertility of the land. This recipe incorporates the leaves of the grapevine, flesh (try to use hormone-free, free-range beef), and a little bit of wine, so all the elements are present. With its Dionysian association and the fact that it is a hearty and grounding dish, this is a great dish to serve at a festive occasion or ritual where wild ecstatic rites are enacted freely.

Having to roll each grape leaf bundle by hand is a great opportunity to let your mind wander in the ritualism, meditatively blessing the food. So, after the loving and trance-evoking effect of putting this interesting dish together, and while nibbling a few leaves and sipping some good red Chianti, let your mind drift back to the days of the Maenads.

The Maenads were seen as sacred madwomen. They enjoyed uninhibited sex, dancing, drinking, and singing totally free of persecution. According to some historical literature, it was possible for women who had become so worn down by life's pressures to run reckless and free with the wild-haired priestesses of Dionysus. On their return, no questions were asked, and the women's dignity remained intact.

Picture yourself running naked through the groves, pursuing the sacred stag with your sister priestesses. See the ancient bonfires and unbridled jubilation of life, death, and rebirth. Be inspired, remember your connections to the earth and all living things, and rejoice.

This recipe and introduction comes to us from Victoria Bearden, a renowned psychic and astrologer for twenty years. Her background includes both Eastern and Western mysticism, Wiccan and esoteric practices, and she is part Greek.

==

1 (16-OUNCE) JAR GRAPE LEAVES

1¼ POUNDS GROUND BEEF

1 MEDIUM ONION, CHOPPED

1 CUP INSTANT RICE, UNCOOKED

½ TEASPOON GROUND CAYENNE
PEPPER (OPTIONAL)

HANDFUL OF CURRANTS
(OPTIONAL)

1 LARGE EGG

¼ CUP CHOPPED FRESH PARSLEY

¼ CUP CHOPPED FRESH MINT

HANDFUL OF PINE NUTS
(OPTIONAL)

SALT AND PEPPER

1 (15-OUNCE) CAN WHOLE
TOMATOES

2¼ CUPS BEEF BROTH

SPLASH OF CHIANTI OR OTHER
RED WINE

½ CUP WATER

Since they are pickled, grape leaves must be removed from the jar and immersed in cool water for approximately 5 to 10 minutes to cleanse the excess brine. While the leaves are soaking, mix together the ground beef, onion, rice, ground cayenne pepper, currants, egg, parsley, mint, and pine nuts in a large bowl. Salt and pepper to taste. The amount of rice may vary in accordance to your individual preference. Make sure the mixture sticks well together and is not too wet.

On a large cutting board, or other clean surface, line up a few leaves at a time, shiny side down. Pinch or cut off the stem at the top of each leaf. Place approximately 1 tablespoon of the filling in the center of each leaf. Shape the filling into an oval horizontally across the surface of the leaf. Fold the side flaps inward, then roll them tightly upward, toward the tapered end. The stickiness of the meat mixture will help hold them together. All the filling should be covered within the leaf.

Using a large, heavy stew pot, carefully arrange each rolled leaf side by side, in layers, until they are neatly packed and you still have about 2 inches of headroom. As you are stacking, crush some of the canned tomatoes in your hand and disperse in between the layers of rolled leaves. When the pot is full, add the remaining juice from the tomatoes, beef broth, wine, and water. Adjust your liquid so the level reaches the top layer of leaves but does not cover them completely. Place a heavy plate on top of the leaves to hold them in place while cooking.

Bring to a boil, reduce the heat, and simmer. Cook for 45 to 50 minutes. Remember not to lift the cover so as to not relieve the pressure. When done, the rice will be fully cooked, there will be little to no pinkness to the meat, and the leaves will be tender. As the rolled leaves are intended to be eaten with the fingers, be sure to let them cool before serving.

This dish is traditionally served with chilled yogurt on the side. Stuffed grape leaves can be served as a side dish or even a main course.

Note: You may substitute approximately 2 cups of the steamed rice of your choice for the instant rice. Only cook it for about half the required time, though, as the rice will continue to cook with the recipe.

KITCHERI

Serves 4

1 CUP BASMATI RICE

1/2 CUP SPLIT YELLOW MUNG BEANS

3 TABLESPOONS OIL (OLIVE, SESAME, OR SUNFLOWER)

1 TABLESPOONS MUSTARD SEEDS

1 TABLESPOON CUMIN SEEDS

1 TEASPOON MASALA

1 TEASPOON TURMERIC

1 1/2 TEASPOONS SALT

2 TABLESPOONS COCONUT FLAKES

1/2 CUP *EACH* CARROTS, PARSNIPS, RED POTATOES, CHOPPED

3 CUPS WATER

4 TABLESPOONS GHEE

A staple in Ayurvedic cooking, kitcheri is the primary food in Panchakarma, an Ayurvedic cleansing and antiaging therapy used to promote longevity, self-reliance, strength, energy, vitality, mental clarity, deep relaxation, and overall well-being. According to Ayurvedic principles, health is achieved by living in harmony with nature and the five elements: fire, water, air, earth and ether, which are expressed in the three life forces known as doshas: vata, pitta, and kapha. The three doshas are defined as follows: vata personalities are wiry, small-boned, nervous, and quick-tempered; pitta types are medium-boned, strong, determined, and even-tempered; kapha types are athletic, stocky, and generally easy-going.

This kitcheri recipe is beneficial for all three dosha types. It is particularly helpful during fall, as this transitory season is sometimes stressful with its unpredictable weather patterns. The moisturizing combination of mung beans, rice, and ghee found in kitcheri balance the drying and depleting effects of autumn. Also, this nourishing stew is easy on the digestive system.

This recipe was donated by Pilar Chandler, an Ayurevedic doctor, herbalist, and massage therapist. She lives, works, and teaches in southern California.

Rinse and soak the rice and beans in water for at least 5 to 6 hours, or overnight. Rinse again, and drain. Heat the oil in a large, heavy-bottomed pan. Over medium-high heat, sauté the mustard seeds, cumin, masala, and tumeric for 3 to 4 minutes. When the mustard seeds begin to pop, lower the heat to medium. Add the rice, beans, salt, coconut, carrots, parsnips, and potatoes. Sauté for an additional 5 minutes. Add the water to the pan, and stir. Cover and cook over medium/low heat, or until the rice and beans are cooked, about 15 to 20 minutes. Garnish each serving with a dollop of ghee.

Parsley and Potato Soup

Serves 6

2 TABLESPOONS BUTTER

1 ONION, COARSELY CHOPPED

CHOPPED STEMS FROM 1 BUNCH
WATERCRESS

1/3 CUP CHOPPED FRESH PARSLEY

4 RUSSET POTATOES, PEELED AND
QUARTERED

CHICKEN BROTH

SALT AND PEPPER

1 CUP HEAVY WHIPPING CREAM

The Autumnal Equinox begins the season for going within, introspection, and self-evaluation. Therefore, during this season, Wiccans choose to eat those foods that grow underground, such as potatoes. The potato has long been a mainstay of Irish foods and rates only second to corn in Native American cuisine.

Potato is believed to be a complete food because it possesses a high content of potassium, ion, vitamins B and C, and riboflavin. The potassium alleviates heart troubles and produces elastic tissue and supple muscle. As potatoes are high in starch and easy on the kidneys, potato soup is a favorite curative soup for kidney and stomach disorders. Parsley also offers a wide range of advantages such as being high in iron; it is helpful to the kidneys and supportive of the sexual system.

In a large saucepan, melt 1 tablespoon of the butter over medium heat. Add the onion and sauté until tender. Add the watercress stems and parsley and cook until tender. Add the potatoes and enough broth to cover. Season with salt and pepper. Cook for 45 minutes, until the potatoes are soft.

Pour the mixture into a blender and purée. Return to the pan and boil briskly for a few minutes, stirring constantly. Add the remaining butter and the whipping cream, and simmer for 3 minutes.

Remove from heat and check for desired consistency. If the soup is too thick, add more chicken broth to thin it out. Mix in 1/4-cup increments until the soup reaches preferred consistency. (If it is too thin, remove about 1/2 cup of the soup, and using a wire whisk, mix 1/4 cup of flour into the soup, mixing until smooth. If you add flour, allow to cook for 5 to 10 more minutes. Pour into soup bowls.

Enchanting Grape Salad

Serves 4

1 CUP SHREDDED SPINACH OR
BUTTER LEAF LETTUCE

1½ CUPS GREEN GRAPES

1 CUP DICED GREEN APPLES

½ CUP CRUMBLED FETA CHEESE

¼ CUP BALSAMIC VINEGAR

Grapes have traditionally been used throughout the world for their curative purposes. Due to their high magnesium content, grapes are a natural diuretic. In addition, the grape has a soothing quality, which helps calm the nervous system.

In Spain, the Fiesta de la Vendimia honors the grape harvest and is held from September 20 to 27. The fiesta centers in Logroño, the capital of the La Rioja region in northwestern Spain. La Rioja has the perfect climate for cultivating grapes, as well as good moisture plenty of sun, and porous soil. It is also believed that Dionysus, also known as Bacchus, reigns supreme in La Rioja's vineyards.

During this commemoration of the grape harvest, everything is sacred. Each task—from harvesting and trimming the vines, to the glassblowing craft and the making of baskets, barrels, and *botas* (wineskins)—takes on magical significance. The Fiesta de la Vendimia begins when the first wine of the year is offered to and blessed by the Virgin of Valvanera on the riverside of Espolón de Logroño. Afterward, participants celebrate with colorful processions, bullfights, flamenco dancing, fireworks, food, and wine tasting. Offer the grapes in this salad to the Great Goddess and, if possible, party in a vineyard with passion and abandon.

Combine the lettuce, grapes, and apples in a salad bowl. Add the feta cheese and mix the ingredients together. Add the balsamic vinegar and toss. Serve immediately.

Luminous Crescents

32 crescents

6 TABLESPOONS BUTTER, SOFTENED

1 PINT SMALL-CURD COTTAGE CHEESE

1/8 TEASPOON SALT

2 CUPS ALL-PURPOSE FLOUR

1/2 CUP GRATED ROMANO CHEESE

1/2 CUP GRATED PARMESAN CHEESE

The Autumnal Equinox is one of the best times for moon scrying, or divining, because the sky is crystal clear. It is the time to go within and reflect.

Go outside or sit by a window where you have a clear view of the moon. Stare at the moon for at least thirty seconds and then close your eyes. Breathe deeply three times. Ask for clarification of a problem that has been plaguing you. Sit and patiently wait. What was the first thing that popped into your mind? Was it a voice from within or a whisper in the wind? Was it an image? Did you feel anything? The more you trust in yourself, the easier the process will become.

The moon receives her light from Father Sun. All her purity and grace she reflects on you. Go forth and direct that same reflection through the Luminous Crescents onto your loved ones.

Cream the butter, cottage cheese, and salt in a bowl. Add the flour, mixing well until blended. Divide the dough into four flat balls. Wrap in wax paper, and refrigerate until cold enough to roll, approximately 1 hour.

Preheat the oven to 400°. Lightly grease three baking sheets. On a floured sheet of waxed paper, roll out one ball of dough at a time to a 9- or 10-inch round. Sprinkle each round with 1¹/2 tablespoons of the Parmesan cheese and 1¹/2 tablespoons of the Romano cheese. Cut each round into eight pie-shaped wedges. Beginning with the wide end of each wedge, roll toward the point. Place the wedges point-side down, on the prepared baking sheets. Shape into crescents and sprinkle with the remaining cheese. Bake for 20 to 25 minutes, until golden. Immediately loosen from baking sheets and place on wire racks to cool.

Roasted Carrots

Foods that are grown underground have special significance during the Autumnal Equinox. You, along with others, are invited to move inward toward the depths of your being, to go undercover like the carrot. The new moon is symbolic of the darkness before creation, when all things are possible. The new moon of autumn often precedes the harvest full moon, which pagans traditionally acknowledge as the most powerful in helping us attain our needs and desires. Therefore, it stands to reason that the new moon preceding the harvest moon is the most powerful time to excavate concealed or secret gifts.

We all have hidden talents, which are sometimes even our most significant. These abilities represent our true selves and exemplify all we would love to share with our friends and family but are afraid to because of ridicule, failure, or something more devious. To draw out your special gift and the confidence to let it shine in the world, begin with a grounding rite. See yourself as a tree with roots extending to Mother Earth and branches reaching toward Father Sun. Bring in the warmth of the sun and let the energy stretch out toward your toes and go through the soil of the ground. When you feel centered, light a red candle and hold a clear crystal between your hands. Say

Goddess, grant me the strength to see the wisdom of sharing the gift you have given me.
Open my eyes to the confidence already in me to fulfill my destiny.
Help me to erect a shield to protect my fragile self from words of doubt and ridicule.
Remind me of the joy I found as a child and help me to live it every day.
I have a gift to bring to this world.
I have a unique talent no one else has.
I have the power to create the perfect space for my authentic self to shine through.
I am not fulfilling my dream to (fill in your dream).

Serves 4

1 POUND CARROTS

2 1/2 TABLESPOONS OLIVE OIL

2 TEASPOONS WHITE WINE
VINEGAR

2 TEASPOONS CHARDONNAY OR
OTHER WHITE WINE

1 TABLESPOONS MINCED
FRESH PARSLEY

1 TABLESPOON MINCED
FRESH TARRAGON

1/2 TEASPOON MINCED
FRESH MARJORAM

SALT AND PEPPER

Seal the spell by saying

Do good unto all and no harm come to me,
By the will of my highest power,
This spell I cast three times three times three.
So Mote it Be.

Preheat the oven to 400°F. Peel the carrots and place them in a baking dish. Brush the carrots lightly with oil. Roast for 10 to 15 minutes, until golden brown. Slice the carrots and place them on a serving dish. Drizzle the vinegar and wine over the carrots. Sprinkle on the fresh herbs. Season with salt and pepper.

Note: Complementary herbs, such as dill or thyme, may be substituted for parsley, tarragon, and marjoram, according to taste.

Farls

Serves 8

2 CUPS DRY OATS

3 CUPS WARM WATER

3 CUPS MASHED POTATOES

2 TABLESPOONS BUTTER, AT ROOM
TEMPERATURE

1/2 TEASPOON CORNSTARCH

1/2 TEASPOON BAKING POWDER

SALT AND PEPPER

PINCH OF FRESH, MINCED THYME

Farls are also known as potato farrs or potato scones. This delicious potato dish is eaten for breakfast from northern Ireland to Scotland. A ritual that accompanies this popular side dish involves the use of water. Still, dark water is recommended; from the womb of darkness you will uncover your answers. This ritual can provide answers to questions that you have had difficulty answering. Reflect into the depths of a pond, water in a dark bowl, or a tide pool for five to fifteen minutes, or longer, if possible. Set a timer or allow your natural rhythm to tell you when to stop. Get comfortable by placing either a towel or blanket under your knees or bottom and dress warmly. This ritual works best at night or even dusk.

Unfocus your eyes as if you were trying to find the 3-D image in a hologram painting or picture. Relax your mind and allow thoughts to drift in and out of your awareness, without concentrating on any particular image or idea. Try to become effortless in your search, open to solutions and random musings.

Withdraw from the water when you are noticeably uncomfortable, distracted by the world around you, or when the alarm rings. Hopefully, you will have received a message, which may or may not be related to the problem you were trying to solve. The Mother has a way of telling us what we need to know. If you did not get a message, wait a couple of days and see if an answer is revealed to you. If not, try it again a few days later. Alternatively, some people have had success staring into a fire (for this meditation, see page 185).

In a saucepan, soak the oats in the warm water for 15 to 20 minutes, until soft and slightly swollen. Drain off the excess water. Transfer to a large mixing bowl. Add the potatoes, butter, cornstarch, baking powder, salt, pepper, and thyme, mixing well. Knead until the mixture is like thick dough. Form eight round patties. Pour 1/2 inch of oil into a small skillet. Fry the patties until lightly browned. Serve immediately.

Yam Enchiladas

10 to 12 enchiladas

==========

4 TO 6 YAMS

1 MEDIUM RED ONION

2 CLOVES GARLIC, CHOPPED AND MASHED

1¹/₂ TEASPOONS NUTMEG

¹/₂ CUP FINELY CHOPPED FLAT-LEAF PARSLEY

¹/₂ CUP MINCED FRESH CILANTRO

1 (4-OUNCE) CAN BLACK OR GREEN OLIVES, CHOPPED OR SLICED

¹/₂ CUP GRATED SHARP CHEDDAR CHEESE

10 TO 12 MEDIUM FLOUR TORTILLAS

1 (8-OUNCE) CAN GREEN ENCHILADA SAUCE

quash is indigenous to the Western Hemisphere. It was used extensively by the Native Americans of the Southwest and Plains regions centuries before the arrival of the white man. The Taos Indians often used squash blossoms in their basket weaving.

Indians ate with great appreciation and reverence for the foods the Mother provided from Her bountiful harvest. They also believed a happy peaceful cook created healthy dishes that benefited, while negative feelings produced inferior foods or illness.

As you prepare this meal, begin by thanking the Mother for providing for you. Concentrate on happy thoughts. Visualize the joy your family and friends will have after they have eaten a meal prepared with love. Charge even your utensils with positive energy, as these tools are channels of spirit energy.

This recipe was donated by Jean from Sunshine Gardens in Encinitas, California.

Preheat the oven to 375°F. Scrub the yams, but do not peel. Pierce the yams to allow the steam to escape. Bake the yams for 45 minutes, until tender. Remove from the oven and decrease temperature to 350°F. Scoop the yams out of their skins and place in a large bowl. Add the onion, garlic, nutmeg, parsley, cilantro, olives, and half of the cheese, mixing until will combined.

Warm the tortillas by heating in the microwave for 10 seconds or flipping over an open flame on a gas stove until soft and pliable. Place 2 to 3 tablespoons of the yam mixture in the center of each tortilla and roll. When all the mixture has been used, pour the sauce over the tortillas and sprinkle on the remaining cheese. Bake for 40 minutes.

MEDIEVAL GAME BIRD

Serves 4

6 PIECES BACON, CHOPPED

3 CLOVES GARLIC, CHOPPED

4 SMALL GAME BIRDS
(QUAIL, PHEASANT, OR CORNISH
GAME HEN)

1 CUP COARSELY CHOPPED
MUSHROOMS

1/2 TEASPOON COARSELY CHOPPED
ROASTED HAZELNUTS

2 CUPS ALE

3/4 CUP WATER

2 TO 3 BAY LEAVES, CRUMBLED

SALT AND PEPPER

6 THICK SLICES WHEAT BREAD

ame birds are hunted during the fall months when the prey is fattest. During medieval times, the most hunted game bird in northern Europe was the red grouse. The Cornish game hen originated from Cornwall in the southwest tip of England. The light meat of game birds was highly sought after in the Middle Ages. The people came up with a nimble scheme for capturing their favorite fowl.

The custom began in narrow canyons on the moors. The peasants stood in a line with sticks and beat the bushes, moving the birds along the gorge toward a wall of stones. Behind those peasant-built stone walls waited the noblemen with their slings, rocks, nets, or bows and arrows. As the unlucky birds flew past, the hunters took a shot at them. Much later, guns were introduced into this method of hunting. This ancient ritual flushing out game birds for hunting is still practiced today on private hunting grounds in England, Scotland, and Germany.

In the bottom of a heavy pot, fry the bacon and the garlic, until the bacon is lightly browned. Add the birds and brown on all sides. Add the mushrooms and nuts. Continue to cook for a few minutes, then add the ale, water, and bay leaves. Bring to a boil, cover, and simmer gently for 2 to 2 1/2 hours, until the meat is falling off the bone. Remove the birds. Cool the juices completely and remove the excess fat. Remove the meat from the bones when the birds are cool. Return the pieces of meat to the skimmed juices, reheating slowly. Salt and pepper to taste.

Serve the slices of meat on the bread, dribbling on plenty of juice. Include more of the juices and bread with the meal. Salad is a great accompaniment to this dish.

VEGETABLE LAMB SHANKS

Serves 4

4 LAMB SHANKS

2 CLOVES GARLIC, MINCED

SALT AND PEPPER

8 CARROTS, PEELED, CUT INTO
1-INCH PIECES

8 SMALL WHITE ONIONS, CHOPPED

8 CAPS FROM BUTTON
MUSHROOMS

8 SMALL STALKS CELERY, DICED

1/2 CUP FRESH PEAS

1/2 CUP CUT FRESH GREEN BEANS

2 (8-OUNCE) CAN TOMATO SAUCE

Sheep were utilized mainly for their wool in the Middle Ages, and lamb was usually only eaten by aristocrats. The majority of people were not privy to such a treat.

How often have we pined for that which we do not possess? Instead of lamenting over meager means, embrace the bounty you have. There will be many opportunities to learn on the earth plane, and some of these will come from accepting your limitations. By embracing acceptance, you are working in harmony with that which you cannot understand. Focusing on unhappy situations will only increase their power, for that which you concentrate on grows. Whatever you give attention to will flourish.

If you wish to change your environment, relationship, or workplace, try the meditation and let go:

I am the place the Goddess shines through.
She and I are one, not two.
If I remain relaxed and free,
She'll carry out Her plan through me.

Preheat the oven to 350°F. Place the lamb shanks in a large baking dish. Sprinkle the garlic over the lamb shanks. Season with salt and pepper. Bake for 30 minutes, turning frequently to brown on all sides. Add the carrots, onions, mushrooms, celery, peas, green beans, and tomato sauce. Adjust the heat and bake at 375°F for 45 minutes to 1 hour, until meat is tender.

Banana Bread

2 loaves, 20 slices each

1¼ CUPS GRANULATED SUGAR

½ CUP BUTTER, SOFTENED

2 LARGE EGGS

1¾ CUPS MASHED RIPE BANANAS

½ CUP MILK

1½ TEASPOONS VANILLA EXTRACT

2½ CUPS ALL-PURPOSE FLOUR

1 TEASPOON BAKING SODA

1 TEASPOON SALT

As we move into the depths of our soul during this introspective sabbat, we offer this recipe and ritual for manifesting the home of your dreams. A smell of banana bread baking often elicits childhood memories of warmth, comfort, and safety. To manifest the home of your dreams, you must first dispose of all that no longer serves you, such as furniture or restricted ideas of the perfect home.

As you mix the ingredients, make a list of the most important things your home must have. What is it about your surroundings that makes you feel most at home? Light a candle and repeat this saying: "Goddess, direct me to where I can best serve you." In addition, list feelings you would like your new home to emanate. You may want to write this list down three times.

Don't limit yourself and get suck in a game of semantics, only allowing a script of what you want to be satisfactory and acceptable. If it's running water you want, concentrate on water flowing. This desire might turn out to be a stream, a waterfall, or simply a flowing fountain.

Next, ask assistance from your host of guardian angels. Request that your parent or mentor angel move ahead to your new house and with the sweetest love, call you home. Make sure to ask that your companion angel stay close by and give you comfort for those dark and uncertain days while you await the manifestation of your dream.

Lastly, remember to conclude this ritual with a prayer of gratitude. If we say only one word of prayer our whole lives that word should be "thanks."

Preheat the oven to 350°F. Grease the bottoms of two loaf pans, 8½ by 4½ by 2½ inches, with shortening or butter.

In a large bowl, cream the sugar and butter. Add the eggs, and mix. Add the bananas, milk, and vanilla, beating until smooth. In a small bowl, combine the flour, baking soda, and salt. In increments, add the flour mixture to the banana mixture. Pour into the pans. Bake for 1 hour, until a toothpick inserted into the center comes out clean. Cool for 5 minutes in the pans on a wire rack.

Soothing Juniper and Mulled Pears

Serves 4

---

4 FIRM BARTLETT OR ANJOU PEARS

2/3 CUP MERLOT OR OTHER
RED WINE

2/3 CUP PINEAPPLE JUICE

1/3 CUP FIRMLY PACKED DARK
BROWN SUGAR

4 JUNIPER BERRIES, CRUSHED

In addition to being a healing agent for typhoid, cholera, dysentery, tapeworms, and other ills associated with poverty, juniper has long been associated with ritual cleansing and the purifying of the soul.

Now that the dark season is upon us, it is the time to forgive yourself and others for wrongdoings, which will cleanse your consciousness and karma. To err is human and to forgive is Divine. As you prepare this dish, visualize all the negative things you are feeling. Let the emotions build as the mixture simmers. As you baste, visualize anointing yourself with love, free of guilt and sorrow. Charge the food with strength and power, enabling you to be the person you want to be. Bind this spell by visualizing yourself surrounded in white pure light that encases you and protects you from all harm. Now imagine the symbol or image you want to create is encased in this same protective light. Say

> This spell I make true,
> Through love and light.
> Harming none and helping all,
> Is how it shall be.
> By the power of
> Three times three times three.

Peel, core, and quarter the pears. In a saucepan, add the red wine, pineapple juice, brown sugar, and juniper berries. Simmer for 3 minutes. Add the pears. Simmer, uncovered, for 15 minutes, stirring and basting occasionally.

Serve in small decorative bowls or red wine glasses.

Pomegranate Granita

The turning point of the Autumnal Equinox is marked by the harvest, also known as the Witches' Thanksgiving. The weather is changing, the days grow short, and a favorite fruit, the sensual ruby-red pomegranate, appears at the fruit stand.

In much of the ancient world, the pomegranate symbolized the Goddess and fertility, a womb with many seeds, and the blood of life in its crimson juice. Use the beautiful pomegranate in an Autumnal Equinox ceremony to honor the Mother. Cut into the pomegranate with an athame with a white handle and tear it open by hand, squeezing the juice out and letting it drip onto the earth, over the fire, or into the cauldron. We recommend you have a pitcher of Rose Water (page 131) to cleanse the hands afterward. The ravaged fruit can be shared by all the participants, then offered to the fire or given back to Mother Earth, depending on your preference.

While performing this rite, say praises to the Goddess, giving thanks for the harvest, our many blessings, and all that is beautiful in the world. Implore the others in the circle to bow their heads and think about what they are thankful for and what they can sacrifice to help heal Mother Earth or spread positive energy to their family, friends, or community.

The following pomegranate recipe is from Victoria Bearden, an artist, dreamer, wanderer through sacred groves, stargazer, and servant of Goddess.

Serves 4 to 6

2 CUPS FRESH
POMEGRANATE JUICE

1/3 CUP FRESHLY SQUEEZED
ORANGE JUICE OR TANGELO JUICE
(SAVE RIND)

1/2 TEASPOON FRESHLY SQUEEZED
LEMON JUICE (SAVE RIND)

1 TABLESPOON FRESHLY SQUEEZED
GINGER JUICE

1/4 CUP GRANULATED SUGAR

1 ORANGE, MANDARIN ORANGE,
BLOOD ORANGE, OR TANGELO,
SLICED, FOR GARNISH

MINT LEAVES, FOR GARNISH

1/3 CUP FRESH POMEGRANATE
SEEDS, FOR GARNISH

Combine the liquid ingredients and the sugar in a glass container with an airtight cover. Place in the freezer, just until the mixture begins to set, about 45 minutes to 1 hour. Remove from the freezer and scrape with a fork to break up the ice crystals. Return to the freezer and repeat every 20 to 30 minutes as it continues to set and until it achieves a grainy texture.

Make long curly citrus rind strands with a lemon zester or grater. Spoon portions of the sorbet into pretty, chilled glasses (large martini glasses work well). Garnish with citrus slices, 1 to 2 mint leaves per glass, and pomegranate seeds. Serve immediately, because granita melts quickly.

Note: For the pomegranate juice, place the seeds in a blender on medium-high speed, then run through a fine strainer and collect the liquid in a container. Fruits vary in size and juice content, so start with a large fruit and see where that leaves you. You may need three or more fruits for 2 cups. Pick pomegranates that are really ripe, with leathery skin and very red, very sweet seeds. This will make a big difference in the flavor of the juice.

For the ginger juice, use a garlic press to extract the juice.

Witches' Thanksgiving Brew

14 to 16 (1-cup) servings

4 CUPS RED BERRY SOFT DRINK OR
JUICE, FOR GARNISH

4 CUPS FRESHLY SQUEEZED
ORANGE JUICE

1/4 CUP FRESHLY SQUEEZED
LEMON JUICE

8 CUPS APPLE CIDER

1 CUP WATER

1 CUP WHITE GRAPE JUICE

1 1/2 TEASPOONS GROUND
CINNAMON

The apple cider and cinnamon give this delicious drink a crisp autumn flavor. For an added mystical effect, purchase blocks of dry ice and place them under (or behind) the punch bowl. Dry ice is inexpensive and can be purchased from ice suppliers. Never put dry ice directly in the punch, as it is unsafe to consume. Make sure children are supervised around dry ice.

Apples are a favorite treat during the autumnal holiday and can be used in many games before or after your feast. The common pastime of bobbing for apples takes on a new twist when you assign the name of a lover to a particular apple. It is believed that if you can get that apple, you can "get" the loved one.

On the night before serving, pour the berry drink into ice trays (approximately three will suffice).

The next day, in a large punch bowl, mix the orange juice, lemon juice, apple cider, water, white grape juice, and cinnamon together until well blended. Chill in the refrigerator for at least 1 hour before serving.

When the ice cubes are frozen, add them to the witch's brew to look like bloody ice.

SAMHAIN

Samhain (also known as Halloween, Hallowmas, All Hallows' Eve, All Saints' Eve, Festival of the Dead, and the Third Festival of Harvest) is celebrated October 31.

Samhain is the most important of all the sabbats because it is the start of the Witches' New Year. It is also the most misunderstood and feared sabbat. At this time of year, the veil between the two worlds is very thin. The altar is decorated with fall leaves, apples, pomegranates, pumpkin, and squash. Usually the third and final harvest is completed by October 30, and many people stockpile food in preparation for the upcoming winter months.

A way to banish negativity at Samhain is by bowl burning. In this ritual, you can write down on a piece of paper that aspect of your life from which you wish to be freed. Place the paper into a bowl and light it on fire. Then ask the Universe to transform this energy from a negative one into a more positive one, thanking the Divine Source ahead of time.

Other traditions include making a besom, leaving a plate of food outside for the souls of the dead, making masks, wassailing, and the two-thousand-year-old tradition of creating jack-o'-lanterns to frighten away evil spirits. Most importantly, fellow Wiccans remember with peace and love those who have crossed over to the other side.

Herbs and flowers associated with Samhain include acorn, chrysanthemum, deadly nightshade, dittany, ferns, flax, fumitory, hazel, heather, mullein, oak leaves, pumpkin, sage, straw, thistle, and wormwood.

Traditional foods of Samhain include pumpkin pie, apples, cakes for the dead, cranberry muffins and bread, pears, pork, red foods, beans, pomegranates, all grains, beets, turnips, corn, gingerbread, mulled wine, meat dishes, hazelnuts, ale, cider, and herbal teas.

Yam and Acorn Squash Soup

Serves 4

1 TABLESPOON VEGETABLE OIL

1 LARGE VIDALIA OR PURPLE ONION, CHOPPED

5 CUPS YAMS OR SWEET POTATOES, PEELED AND CUBED

1 SMALL ACORN SQUASH, SEEDED AND CUBED

1 3/4 CUPS CHICKEN BROTH

1/4 CUP PLAIN YOGURT

2 TABLESPOONS PUMPKIN SEEDS, TOASTED

1/4 CUP WHOLE MILK

DASH OF SALT

1/4 TEASPOON WHITE PEPPER

1/4 CUP SOUR CREAM, FOR GARNISH

2 TABLESPOONS SLICED ALMONDS, FOR GARNISH

DASH OF GRATED NUTMEG, FOR GARNISH

The acorn squash received its name because its shape is similar to that of the acorn. Acorns represent the growth of the mighty oak tree burgeoning with life, growing all winter long, and flowering in midsummer as the tree of endurance and triumph.

Each of us has a gift to give, which we must share; it is why we came to be. Often so many things are happening at once that life seems like a whirlwind, but there is only one thing that matters—love. As you reflect on this, burn a brown candle for grounding. Meditate on the unique facet of sunshine that you express and can offer to the world.

There is a myth about the acorn people who live in an ancient oak tree in the center of a very old forest. Everyone, from the ages of five to ninety-five, wears a watch that flashes one simple word—Now. Those younger and older don't need to wear the watch, as they instinctively know to live each day in the present. Each acorn person has a gift that is recognized, nurtured, shared, and honored by the whole community. All love unconditionally, allowing themselves to receive love from others, never judging or condemning.

The acorn people have scattered their acorns to the winds. Their hope is that when every acorn is found, all people will come to understand and commit themselves to the only thing that matters—Love.

Heat the oil in a large saucepan over medium heat. Add the onion; sauté until the onion is golden. Add the yams, squash, and broth. Decrease heat and simmer, covered, until the vegetables are tender, about 25 minutes. Let the mixture cool.

In increments, place the vegetable mixture and yogurt in a blender or food processor. Whirl until puréed. Return the mixture to the saucepan. Add the pumpkin seeds. Stir in the milk to the desired consistency. Season with salt and white pepper. Cook over low heat until heated through, about 5 minutes. Transfer the soup to warmed bowls. Top each serving with a dollop of sour cream and a sprinkle of almonds and nutmeg.

Chicken–Barley Stew with Herbs

Serves 8

2 TABLESPOONS BUTTER

2 CUPS COARSELY CUT GREEN
ONIONS, ALL PARTS

4 CLOVES GARLIC, MINCED

2 TO 3 POUNDS CHICKEN BREASTS,
ON THE BONE

3/4 CUP BARLEY

3 TABLESPOONS RED WINE
VINEGAR

3 3/4 CUPS WATER

2 BAY LEAVES, CRUSHED

2 TABLESPOONS MINCED
FRESH SAGE

A heat producer, barley stew is a delicious main dish during the colder months of fall and winter when we can all use some extra warmth. Barley was also a common medieval remedy for acute ailments. Often nothing else but barley gruel was given to the patient until the crisis was over.

To produce the most curative effects, it is best to work with nature and harmony. Wiccans create by following the path of the sun, so it follows that you must stir food in a clockwise direction. To flow with nature is survival. Allow the ebb and flow of life to cascade over you without any more attachment than a casual observer. You are not the events of your life but a culmination of the attitudes in response to situations and your environment.

As you learn to align yourself on the deeper levels of the natural world, you will be pleased to discover there is a greater plan, a greater love than you ever conceived possible. You are loved beyond your capacity to understand. All is well.

Melt the butter in a large Dutch oven or a heavy pot with a lid. Add the green onions and garlic; sauté. Add the chicken and cook until browned on all sides. Stir in the barley, vinegar, water, and bay leaves. Bring to a boil, then decrease heat and simmer for 1 to 1 1/2 hours.

Remove the chicken and let it cool. Remove the meat from bones and add it to the soup. Mix in the sage, stirring well.

Note: You may substitute 1 cup celery chopped in 1-inch pieces for the green onions. You can also use boneless, skinless chicken breasts.

Onion Shortcake

9 squares

2 CUPS ALL-PURPOSE FLOUR

4 TEASPOONS BAKING POWDER

1¹/₂ TEASPOONS SALT

4 TABLESPOONS VEGETABLE
SHORTENING

²/₃ CUP MILK

2 TABLESPOONS BUTTER

2¹/₂ CUPS SLICED ONIONS

1 LARGE EGG

¹/₂ CUP LIGHT CREAM

PAPRIKA, FOR GARNISH

POPPY SEEDS, FOR GARNISH

Samhain is the time to contemplate what we have reaped, all the goodness that has come to us, obstacles we have overcome, and desires we have manifested.

Bring some Onion Shortcake to a circle during a Samhain gathering of good friends and close family members. Beginning with the host, have the guests share what they are grateful for, working clockwise around the circle. As each person shares, invite him or her to take a piece of bread. This is symbolic of allowing the gift to become a part of one's whole being, ingesting the gifts from above, and enabling these offerings to feed the body. If someone is not comfortable speaking aloud, have him or her think about it or write it down.

Speaking of or writing down your appreciation does two things. First, it helps you remember all the good that has been bestowed upon you. You may come to recognize how often your dreams came true—especially once you applied yourself and took the necessary steps to make it happen. Second, by showing your gratitude and giving thanks, you are sending love outward. Remember, whatever good you do comes back to you three times. Often we are rewarded with additional abundance when we acknowledge the Goddess's kindness and give thanks.

This recipe, along with four others, comes to us from Terrie Hurt. Terrie has a master's degree in early modern European history, specializing in witchcraft. Her family has collected and read hundreds of recipes over the generations and they all love to cook!

Preheat the oven to 400°F. Sift together the flour and baking powder with ¹/₂ teaspoon of the salt. Cut in the shortening. Add the milk and knead the dough lightly. Flatten into a greased 8 by 8-inch casserole dish.

Melt the butter in a skillet and sauté the onions, until golden. Let the onions cool, then spread them over the dough.

Beat the egg, cream, and the remaining salt. Pour over the onions. Sprinkle with the paprika and poppy seeds. Bake for 15 to 20 minutes.

Apple Scones

3 dozen scones

1 APPLE, ANY VARIETY

2 CUPS ALL-PURPOSE FLOUR

2 TABLESPOONS GRANULATED SUGAR

3 TEASPOONS BAKING POWDER

1/2 TEASPOON GROUND CINNAMON

1/2 TEASPOON SALT

6 TABLESPOONS VEGETABLE SHORTENING

1/2 CUP RAISINS

1/4 CUP APPLE JUICE

As you prepare the apple for this dish, why not try divining your romantic future? Peel an apple in one long, unbroken strip, as best you can. Throw the resulting strip of peel over your shoulder. The first initial of the future spouse can be divined by the formation of the apple peel, using your imagination, of course. Or get an idea of future marital bliss by cutting an apple in half and counting the seeds. While you do so, think about the love you want to manifest. If there is an even number of seeds, marriage is in the near future. If one of the seeds is cut, you are headed for a stormy relationship; if two seeds are cut, widowhood.

Slice an apple in half to see the two shapes it forms. If you cut the apple crosswise, the seeds form a pentacle, otherwise known as the witch's star and an important symbol of the Wiccan religion. It symbolizes feminine energy, including earth, while each of the five points represents a vast array of ideas and possibilities: the elements of earth, wind, fire, and air or the four directions and the fifth component, which is the Spirit or essence of truth. If you cut the apple lengthwise, the seeds form a heart, representative of the unconditional love the Goddess holds for all.

Peel, core, and mince the apple. Preheat the oven to 400°F. In a bowl, mix the flour, sugar, baking powder, cinnamon, and salt. With a pastry blender, cut in the shortening. Stir in the apples and raisins. Add the apple juice to stiffen the dough.

Turn the dough out onto a floured surface. Roll the dough to about 1/2 inch thick. Cut into triangles. Bake on an ungreased baking sheet for 10 minutes, until light brown.

Baked Butternut Squash

Serves 6

1 MEDIUM BUTTERNUT OR
ACORN SQUASH

2 TABLESPOONS BUTTER AT ROOM
TEMPERATURE

1/2 CUP FRESHLY SQUEEZED
ORANGE JUICE

DASH OF GROUND CINNAMON

inter squash is at its highest seasonal peak during the Samhain season. Use a squash in this ceremony to pay tribute to the deceased, the most important event of the Samhain celebration.

After you scrape out the squash, take the hollowed shell and use it for this gratitude ritual that honors the dead. Place a thick votive candle in the center of the squash. Make sure the candle you use is taller than the squash by a couple of inches. Light the candle. Cast a circle to protect you and your guests from unwanted intruders by visualizing the flame encircling you all. Personally welcome all the loving spirits and teachers who have guided you. Hand each of your guests a candle. Ask your guests to light their candles from the center candle one at a time. As they do this, invite them to acknowledge and give thanks for their mentors and loved ones who have crossed over to the other side.

Preheat the oven to 350°F. Cut the squash in half, and scoop out the seeds, scraping clean. Place the squash in a shallow baking dish. Dot each half with butter. Drizzle the orange juice and sprinkle the cinnamon over the squash. Bake, uncovered, for 30 to 45 minutes, or until you can easily put a fork in the squash. Slice each half into 3 equal portions and serve.

Stuffed Pumpkin

In keeping with Samhain customs, we include pumpkins, as they are associated with this New Year celebration. The custom of the jack-o'-lantern made out of hollowed-out turnips or beets came from Ireland. Immigrants to America later used pumpkins and squash. According to the legend, the jack-o'-lantern derived its name from a man named Jack, a mischievous man, who eluded the devil's attempts to steal his soul many times. When Jack died, he could not get into heaven because of his roguish ways. He went to the gates of hell, and the devil also refused him entrance. Instead, the devil tossed out a piece of coal, jokingly offering Jack a means to find his way in the dark. Jack cleverly placed the coal in a turnip, and the makeshift lantern provided his light as he wandered about purgatory. To ward off dark, unwanted, or evil spirits, Wiccans still place a light in a hollowed-out pumpkin or squash, which are strategically located by the front door or in any other passageway in need of protection and light.

Sheryl Axline donated this recipe. Sheryl is deeply committed to ecological causes and living in tune with the natural world. She extends her commitment to healthful living and cooking.

Continues on next page

Serves 8

1 PUMPKIN OR HUBBARD SQUASH,
8 TO 10 INCHES IN DIAMETER

1 TEASPOON SALT

2 TABLESPOONS VEGETABLE OIL

2¹/₂ POUNDS GROUND TURKEY

1 TEASPOON POULTRY SEASONING

1 TEASPOON WHITE PEPPER

2 GOLDEN BELL PEPPERS, CHOPPED

1 LARGE RED ONION, CHOPPED

¹/₃ POUND CHOPPED PRECOOKED
TURKEY SAUSAGE

2 TEASPOONS OLIVE OIL

2 TEASPOONS MINCED FRESH
OREGANO

2 TEASPOONS VINEGAR

1 TEASPOON GROUND BLACK PEPPER

4 CLOVES GARLIC, PRESSED

1¹/₄ CUPS GOLDEN RAISINS

¹/₃ CUP CHOPPED GREEN PIMENTO-
STUFFED OLIVES

1 (14-OUNCE) CAN SKINNED
TOMATOES, CHOPPED

3 LARGE EGGS, BEATEN

With a sharp knife, cut a circular top, about 5 inches in diameter out of the pumpkin. Save this top for the lid. Scoop out the seeds and scrape the inside of the pumpkin clean. (Save the seeds, sprinkle them with a bit of celery salt, and toast them under the oven broiler for a snack while cooking!)

Fill an extra-large saucepan with about 8 cups of water, adding ¹/₄ teaspoon of the salt. Place the pumpkin in the pot and add another ¹/₄ teaspoon of the salt to the water. The idea is to surround the pumpkin with water and fill it with water, so that it boils from both the outside and inside. (Alternatively, if you have an electric cooking coil, place it inside the pumpkin to boil the water inside the pumpkin.) Cover the pot. Bring the water to a boil, then simmer until the pumpkin meat is almost tender when pierced with a fork, about 15 minutes (the pumpkin should stay firm enough to hold its shape well). Carefully remove the pumpkin from the hot water, drain it well, and dry the outside.

In a large frying pan, heat the vegetable oil. Add the turkey, poultry seasoning, white pepper, bell peppers, and onions. Cook over medium heat, stirring occasionally, just until the turkey is no longer pink. Remove the pan from the heat.

In a large bowl, mix together the turkey sausage, olive oil, oregano, vinegar, black pepper, ¹/₂ teaspoon of salt, and garlic. Add the sausage mixture to the turkey, along with the raisins, olives, and tomatoes, mixing well. Cover the pan and cook over low heat for 15 minutes, stirring occasionally. Remove from heat and allow to cool slightly. Mix the eggs in thoroughly.

Fill the cooked pumpkin with stuffing, pressing the stuffing lightly to pack it. Cover the pumpkin opening with aluminum foil. Place the pumpkin in a greased baking pan and bake at 350°F for 1 hour. When 20 minutes are remaining, replace the foil with the pumpkin lid.

After removing the pumpkin from the oven, spoon off the excess moisture from the top of the stuffing. Allow to cool for 10 to 15 minutes before serving.

To serve, slice the pumpkin from the top to the bottom in fat wedges. Lift each serving onto a dinner place and spoon more of the filling over the top. The entire pumpkin is edible.

Note: You can use red or green peppers; golden, white, or purple bell peppers have a more mellow flavor.

Magickal Mushrooms

12 stuffed mushrooms

2 TABLESPOONS BUTTER

1/4 CUP CHOPPED MUSHROOM STEMS

2 TABLESPOONS DICED GREEN BELL PEPPER

2 TABLESPOONS CHOPPED ONION

3/4 CUP BREAD CRUMBS

2 TABLESPOONS COOKED, CRUMBLED BACON

1 TEASPOON MINCED FRESH ROSEMARY

SALT AND PEPPER

1 CUP LARGE MUSHROOMS, STEMMED

1/3 CUP GRATED CHEDDAR CHEESE

Samhain is the time to remember all of the lessons learned over the past year. Rosemary, an essential ingredient to this side dish, symbolizes remembrance.

As you slice and dice the vegetables for this entrée, reflect on the obstacles you thought you would never surmount and live to tell about. Allow yourself to relish the fact that not only did you survive, but you also did so with flying colors. If you look hard enough, and sometimes it's not so difficult to find, you can uncover the lessons the Goddess had intended for you to learn. You may just be able to see how it has made you stronger, yet gentler, born from your newfound appreciation for the fragility of life.

Rosemary, as an essential oil, can be burned, allowing you to benefit from some of its other properties, such as its warming effects. It will also bring increased alertness and mental clarity. As an herbal remedy, rosemary has been used for depression, nervous diseases, and treating headaches, insomnia, and mental fatigue.

Preheat the oven to 350°F. In a saucepan, melt 1 tablespoon of the butter over low heat. Add the mushroom stems, green pepper, and onions. Sauté until tender. Mix in the bread crumbs, bacon, and rosemary. Season with salt and pepper.

Spoon the mixture into the mushroom caps. Place the caps on a baking sheet. Melt the remaining butter and drizzle it over the caps. Top each mushroom with grated cheddar cheese. Bake for 15 minutes. Serve hot.

Eclectic Eggplant

Serves 6

2 EGGPLANTS, ABOUT
1 POUND EACH

ALL-PURPOSE FLOUR

1 LARGE EGG

1 TABLESPOON OLIVE OIL

SALT AND PEPPER

SEASONED DRY BREAD CRUMBS

3 PLUM TOMATOES, SLICED

3/4 CUP SHREDDED MOZZARELLA
CHEESE

 ggplant is native to India, where it has been cultivated for thousands of years. This vegetable, which belongs to the potato family, contains a large proportion of water.

Water is a great master for those of us who would control the world if we were just given the reins. The ebb and flow of the waves, the disastrous forces of too much accumulated energy as in hurricanes, typhoons, and tsunamis, and the peaceful serenity of a calm lake are all evidence of the Mother showing us how to live a life attuned to nature. The lake gives us an example of quietness in our souls, and the hurricane portrays how we need to distribute our energies. The waves, which are affected by the moon, illustrate how to allow life to recede and expand and learn to flow with its abundance.

When the moon is waxing, becoming full, or when the tide is high, the time is ripe to ask for all you want to accumulate. Visualize all your dreams coming true and your needs being effortlessly met. When the moon is waning, becoming smaller, or when the tide is low, cut away all excess from your life. For example, you can donate clothing you no longer wear, organize a closet or the junk drawer, or roll up all your spare change and cash it in. When you work with nature, your efforts will be well rewarded.

Preheat the oven to 400°F. Cut the eggplants into diagonal slices, and coat with flour.

In a large bowl, beat together the egg, oil, salt, and pepper. Dip each eggplant slice into the egg mixture, then cover with the seasoned bread crumbs. Place them in a greased baking pan, and cover with aluminum foil. Pierce foil with a fork to make air vents. Bake for 15 minutes.

Remove the foil. Top each slice of eggplant with a slice of tomato and sprinkle with shredded cheese. Return to the oven and bake, uncovered, for 10 minutes longer, until the cheese is bubbling.

Rosemary Salmon

Serves 4

1/2 CUP MERLOT OR OTHER
RED WINE

2 TEASPOONS CIDER VINEGAR

2 TEASPOONS CHOPPED FRESH
ROSEMARY

1/4 TEASPOON GROUND GINGER

4 (6-OUNCE) FRESH SALMON
STEAKS

SALT AND PEPPER

2 TABLESPOONS UNSALTED BUTTER

Salmon's red color is associated with Samhain, the time when the old god dies and his blood is spilled, allowing rebirth. The color red also denotes the blood ties of family members. By preparing red foods, you are calling to departed family members, and remembering them. Salmon are also the symbol for determination; swimming upstream to spawn and die is an example for us all to trust the Goddess and Her will. This tenacity is similar to Freya, the goddess of physical love and fertility who ensures that the sexual desire never dies. The salmon's fight to spawn is played with courage and fierceness; it embodies Freya's unparalleled lovemaking prowess and her warrior nature.

According to Norse mythology, Freya was the queen of the war maidens and personally chose which men would accompany her to Valhalla, the warriors' prestigious afterlife. Her hearty strength and unwavering libido made her a powerful woman. Her prized possession was an amber necklace named Brisingamen.

Freya's day, or Friday, is the perfect day to prepare this dish. Enjoy a glass of wine while you cook. Revel in your own sexual nature and pour all that emotion into the sauce. This is your elixir. When you are feeling dowdy, frumpy, unappealing, timid, or weak, wear some amber jewelry or rub a piece of the gem between your fingers. Imagine that you possess the prowess and confidence of Freya.

Set the oven to broil. Mix the wine, vinegar, rosemary, and ginger in a saucepan. Simmer over low heat for at least 10 minutes. The mixture will boil down a bit, but if too much of the wine evaporates, add a little water.

Season both sides of the fish steaks with salt and pepper. Melt butter and brush on the fish.

Set the salmon on a rack in the broiler pan; broil for 9 to 11 minutes. To test for doneness, place a fork in the thickest part of the fish. Gently twist the fork; when the fish flakes easily it is ready. If you prefer fish on the rare side, with a slight pinkness in the middle, remove the fish when the outer part of the thickest point is still a little rare. It will continue to cook after it is removed from the broiler. When the fish is done, place it on a platter, pour the sauce over the fish, and serve

Pumpkin–Praline Pie

1 pie, serving 8

13/4 CUPS COOKED AND
MASHED PUMPKIN

1/2 TEASPOON SALT

11/2 CUPS EVAPORATED MILK

2/3 CUP FIRMLY PACKED LIGHT
BROWN SUGAR

2 TABLESPOONS GRANULATED
SUGAR

13/4 TEASPOONS GROUND
CINNAMON

1/2 TEASPOON GROUND GINGER

1/2 TEASPOON GRATED NUTMEG

1/4 TEASPOON GROUND CLOVES

2 LARGE EGGS

9-INCH FROZEN PIECRUST
(SEE VARIATION)

WHIPPED CREAM, FOR GARNISH

Another popular custom of Samhain involves hiding objects in a dessert for guests to find. After this pie is baked, but before you add whipped cream, cut the pie into eight slices. Hide a ring in one of the slices. Hide two coins and two marbles in four other slices, which leaves two slices with nothing in them.

Before you invite your guests to partake of this dessert, warn them of what they may find in their pie. If they find a ring, marital bliss is theirs. If they discover a coin, wealth is in their future. If they find a marble, this game has predicted a cold and lonely year for them. If they get no treat in their pie slice, their future is sure to be filled with uncertainty and untold possibilities.

With a sharp knife, cut a circular top out of the pumpkin. Scoop out the seeds and scrape the inside of the pumpkin clean. Cut the pumpkin into pieces and peel it like a potato, using either a peeler or a knife. Boil the pieces like you would potatoes for mashing. When soft, drain and mash the pumpkin. Measure 13/4 cups for the pie filling.

Preheat the oven to 425°F. Beat the pumpkin, salt, milk, brown sugar, sugar, and spices together until smooth, using the low speed on a hand mixer or using a wire whisk. Beat the eggs separately, then add them to the mixture. If you can't get the mixture to blend smoothly by whisk or mixer, pour the ingredients into a blender and purée for 30 seconds. Pour the mixture into the piecrust. Bake for 15 minutes. Reduce the oven temperature to 350°F. Bake for 35 minutes longer.

Note: You may substitute 1 (16-ounce) can of pumpkin for the fresh pumpkin.

Topping

1/3 CUP FIRMLY PACKED LIGHT
BROWN SUGAR

1/3 CUP CHOPPED PECANS

1 TABLESPOON BUTTER, AT ROOM
TEMPERATURE

To make the topping, mix the ingredients together. Sprinkle over the pie, leaving a circle in the center bare. Bake for another 10 minutes until a knife inserted into the center comes out clean. In order to avoid a mess, bake this pie by placing the pie pan on a preheated baking sheet. Refrigerate for 4 hours, until chilled. Garnish the center of the pie with a mound of whipped cream. Immediately refrigerate any leftovers after serving.

Variation

If you make your own piecrust (page 207), roll the leftover pastry and cut it into thin shapes of stars, moons, acorns, leaves, etc. Bake for a few minutes, until brown, while the pie is cooling. Place the shapes on each piece of pie for serving.

Molasses–Ginger Animal Cookies

After presenting the offerings to the God (usually cornmeal) and Goddess (a liquid such as apple or passion-fruit juice is a good choice), it is always kind and well received to give these cookies to your guests near the end of your Samhain celebration. Animal cookies are eaten to thank the animals for the food, messages, and beauty they bring us. According to many earth-based religions, each animal offers gifts and qualities that symbolize the strengths we can tap into. These cookies also bring to mind the shape-shifting abilities of Cerridwin, a Celtic variant of the Goddess. Cerridwin changes from Maiden to Mother to Crone throughout the turn of the Wheel, as well as possesses the talent of changing her form to any animal she chooses.

Pass the cookies around to a circle of guests, in a clockwise manner, inviting each guest to name the animal he or she has received. Meanings may be looked up in various books or use one's own intuitive meaning. Here are some examples:

BEAR *brings healing, prophetic dreams, or increased intuition.*

DEER *brings spiritual knowledge and graceful strength, and leads us to Faeryland.*

BUTTERFLY *brings transformation, beauty, and joy.*

RABBIT *brings hidden teachings, and quickness of thought and actions, and tends to bring our worst fear to the forefront, while giving us strength to conquer this false evidence appearing real (fear).*

SQUIRREL *says to plan ahead and balance work and play.*

SNAKE *brings sensuality, enables you to let go of old, no-longer-needed things to make room for the new, and represents the seven chakras, or energy centers, within your being.*

DOLPHIN *brings brings deep wisdom, harmony, playfulness, and the reminder to be cognizant of breath.*

BAT *allows you to overcome blocks and brings knowledge of past lives.*

WOLF *brings protection, knowledge, represents the pathfinder, and reminds you to mark your territory.*

About 3 dozen cookies

3/4 CUP VEGETABLE SHORTENING

1 CUP GRANULATED SUGAR

1/4 CUP LIGHT MOLASSES

1 LARGE EGG

2 1/2 CUPS ALL-PURPOSE FLOUR

2 TEASPOONS BAKING SODA

1/4 TEASPOON GROUND CLOVES

1/4 TEASPOON GRATED NUTMEG

1/2 TEASPOON GROUND GINGER

1 TEASPOON GROUND CINNAMON

1/2 TEASPOON SALT

CONFECTIONERS' SUGAR OR
ICING, FOR GARNISH

CAT *is a signal that you can and will land on your feet.*
FROG *says it is okay to try and releases you from holding onto emotions.*
TURTLE *represents the womb of the Mother.*

Jeanette Reynolds includes these cookies in her Samhain ceremonial circles. Samhain is known as the meat harvest, but since Jeanette is a vegetarian, she has introduced this clever dish as a means of embracing the meat-eating harvest.

Melt the shortening in a saucepan over low heat. Add the sugar and molasses. Lightly beat the egg and add it to the mixture, stirring well. Transfer to a large bowl.

In a small bowl, mix the flour, baking soda, salt, and spices, stirring until well blended. Add to the molasses mixture, mixing well. Chill for 1 to 2 hours.

Preheat the oven to 350°F. Roll the dough on lightly floured waxed paper, adding flour to the dough and roller as needed. Roll the dough to a thickness of about 1/4 inch. Lightly grease 3 baking sheets. Cut the cookies with cookie cutters, dipping the cutters in flour each time you cut a cookie. Place the cookies on the baking sheets. Sprinkle the cookies lightly with sugar (unless you will be decorating them with icing). Bake the cookies for 8 to 10 minutes, watching carefully to make sure the gremlins or pixies don't cause them to burn!

Remove the cookies from the baking sheets and transfer them onto wire racks. Let cool for 5 minutes. If you like, embellish the cookies with icing or confectioners' sugar, which will please the faeries, who love any treat that is sweet and creamy.

All Hallows' Eve Cakes

About 3 dozen cakes

1/2 CUP VEGETABLE OIL

4 OUNCES UNSWEETENED BAKING
CHOCOLATE, MELTED

2 CUPS GRANULATED SUGAR

4 LARGE EGGS

2 TEASPOONS VANILLA EXTRACT

2 CUPS SIFTED CAKE FLOUR

2 TEASPOONS BAKING POWDER

1/2 TEASPOON SALT

1 CUP CONFECTIONERS' SUGAR

Samhain is also known as All Hallows' Eve or Halloween, among other names. Halloween got its start in Ireland around the fifth century. The Celts celebrated the end of the summer on October 31, which is also the time of year when those who have crossed to the other side are remembered. The veil between the two worlds is very thin on Halloween night. On this night, it is a pagan tradition to offer cakes for the dead, to keep them from causing mischief and to show respect and affection for them.

In order to ward off evil spirits, circle your home three times walking backward and counterclockwise before the sun sets. Alternatively, say a prayer that you won't be bothered by naughty lost souls.

On a more positive note, you may want to try the following: As you mix the ingredients for these cakes, reflect on your loved ones who have passed on. Place pictures of the deceased on or beside a north-facing wall. Light a candle and remember the gifts they offered.

In a large bowl, mix the vegetable oil, chocolate, and granulated sugar. Add the eggs, one at a time, stirring well after each addition. Mix in the vanilla. In a small bowl, mix the flour, baking powder, and salt. Stir the flour mixture into the oil mixture. Chill for at least 4 hours or overnight.

Preheat the oven to 350°F. Roll 1 tablespoon of dough into a ball. Coat each ball in confectioners' sugar, rolling until covered. Place the balls about 2 inches apart on a greased baking sheet. Bake for 10 to 12 minutes. The cakes should be soft and the edges should be firm. Do not overbake. They burn easily.

Baked Apples

12 apples

1 DOZEN GOLDEN
DELICIOUS APPLES

1/2 CUP FIRMLY PACKED LIGHT
BROWN SUGAR

3/4 CUP BUTTER, AT ROOM
TEMPERATURE

1 TEASPOON GRATED NUTMEG

1 TEASPOON GROUND CINNAMON

3/4 CUP BOILING WATER

Preheat the oven to 375°F. Peel the upper half of each apple. Core the apples to within 1/2 inch of the bottom. Place the apples in an ungreased baking dish. Place 1 scant tablespoon of the brown sugar, 1 teaspoon of the butter, 1 pinch of the nutmeg, and a pinch of the cinnamon in the center of each apple. Sprinkle the remaining spices over the apples. Add boiling water to the baking dish. Bake for 30 to 40 minutes, basting occasionally. To test for doneness, pierce the apples with a fork. They should be tender.

WASSAIL WICCAN PUNCH

16 to 18 (1-cup) servings

1 CUP WATER

4 CUPS GRANULATED SUGAR

1 TABLESPOON FRESHLY
GRATED NUTMEG

2 TEASPOONS GROUND GINGER

6 WHOLE CLOVES

6 ALLSPICE BERRIES

2 STICKS CINNAMON

1 DOZEN LARGE EGGS, SEPARATED

4 BOTTLES SHERRY OR
MADEIRA WINE

2 CUPS BRANDY

BAKED APPLES (PAGE 173)

Ancient England gave us the custom of wassailing, which is based on the tradition of gathering friends and toasting each other. The Saxon toast "Wass hael!" meant "be whole" or "be well." Draw everyone together in a circle. Place a bowl of Wassail Wiccan Punch or spiced ale in the center. Ladle yourself a cup of the punch. Sip from your glass and shout, "Wass hael!" Pass the glass and implore the guests to take from the bowl and repeat the toast. Alternatively, everyone can toast at the same time.

In being whole, we come to recognize all that we can be and have yet to become. Good health is our Divine right. As a perfect reflection of love, we are whole every day. We just need to see and remember this, especially when we are feeling sick. Here is a toast to your health, both physical and mental:

> *May you be poor in misfortune,*
> *Slow to make enemies,*
> *Fast to make friends,*
> *But rich or poor, slow or fast*
> *May you know nothing but happiness.*

In a large saucepan, combine the water, sugar, and spices. Over medium-high heat, boil for 5 minutes. Beat the egg whites until they stand in soft peaks. In a separate bowl, beat the egg yolks until slightly thickened and paler yellow. Fold the whites into the yolks, using a large heatproof bowl. Quickly strain the sugar and spice mixture through a strainer, to remove larger particles, into the eggs.

In separate pans, bring the wine and the brandy almost to the boiling point. In increments, mix the hot wine and the spice and egg mixture, beginning slowly and stirring briskly with each addition. Toward the end of this process, add the brandy. Add the baked apples just before serving and while the mixture is still foaming.

Note: This also can be made with a combination of beer (a good dark beer is best) and wine, preferably sherry, with roughly 4 parts beer to 1 part sherry.

Pumpkin Juice

Serves 4 to 6

2 CUPS FRESH PUMPKIN, PEELED
AND CHOPPED INTO CHUNKS

2 CUPS APPLE JUICE

1/2 CUP PINEAPPLE JUICE

1 TEASPOON HONEY

2 TABLESPOONS PUMPKIN
PIE SPICE

Candle magic is a relatively easy to practice because we've all been mesmerized by the flickering candle flames from time to time. You can use an engraving tool, a kitchen knife, or a scissor blade to inscribe symbols into the wax of the candle. For example, if you want to draw money to you, etch a dollar sign into your candle. If you wish to unveil secrets within your soul, inscribe the candle with your astrological sign. Or you can design a symbol that is meaningful only to you. After you've inscribed your candle, anoint it with an oil that also represents the desire you hope to manifest, or just use olive oil.

Choose colored candles that are symbolic of the fall season and are associated with your spell. Red represents the Mother, passion, and love. Orange symbolizes creativity and individuality. Yellow means intelligence and wisdom. Gold represents the Father, success, and wealth. Green means prosperity and luck. Burgundy represents desire and the life force. Purple symbolizes nature magic, spirituality, and protection. Or you may choose two candles, one orange and one black, the colors traditionally associated with Samhain—orange to represent the pumpkin harvest and black to symbolize the coming darkness of winter.

As you light the candle, watch the flames and imagine how your life will change once you have manifested your desire. Feel the excitement of expectation blossom within you. As you imagine your desires manifesting, see in your mind's eye the web that unites us all, and feel the contentment that comes from knowing we are all connected.

Purée the pumpkin pieces in a blender or food processor. Add the apple juice and pineapple juice. Add the honey, starting with 1 teaspoon, and adding to the desired sweetness. Blend thoroughly. Sprinkle with the pumpkin pie spice. Chill in the refrigerator for 1 hour. Strain, if the juice is too thick. Serve over ice.

WINTER SOLSTICE

Winter Solstice (also known as Yule, Winter Rite, Midwinter, and Alban Arthan) is celebrated on the first day of winter.

Winter Solstice marks the shortest day of the year. The altar is decorated with mistletoe, holly, and evergreens, such as pine, bay, rosemary, juniper, or cedar. With the solstice, the dead of winter is passing, and you can light a red, orange, or yellow candle as you wait for the coming of light. The Yule log represents the rebirth of God and the returning of the sun. Often a figure of the sun or the God is carved into the Yule log, and sometimes candles are placed into the log as well. The best time of the day to burn a Yule log, traditionally oak or pine, is at dusk.

The Yule tree symbolizes the Cosmic Tree of Life. There are many ways to decorate the Yule tree. Some common garnishes include strings of rosebuds, cinnamon sticks, popcorn, or cranberries, bags of fragrant spices, and quartz crystals hung to look like icicles.

Winter Solstice is the perfect time to create magical charms, which represent desires for the coming year. Such charms include fruits for a good harvest, coins for prosperity, or seeds for fertility. Mistletoe, which is often hung over doorways, is believed to be one of the most powerful healing herbs.

Other traditions that you can follow to celebrate this sabbat include making wreaths, which symbolize the Wheel of Life with no beginning and no ending, and exchanging cookies and sweets with your neighbors.

Herbs and flowers associated with Winter Solstice include bay, bayberry, blessed thistle, cedar chamomile, evergreen, frankincense, holly, ivy, juniper, mistletoe, moss, nutmeg, oak, pinecones, rosemary, and sage.

Traditional foods of Winter Solstice include fruitcakes, nuts, roasted turkey or pork, lambs wool apples, hibiscus or ginger tea, cakes of caraway soaked in cider, red cabbage, apples, oranges, lemons, potato pancakes known as latkes, chestnuts, eggnog, and mulled wine.

Bourbon–Rosemary Almonds

3 cups

3 CUPS WHOLE ALMONDS

1/3 CUP MINCED FRESH ROSEMARY

2 TEASPOONS GROUND CUMIN

1 TEASPOON COARSE SALT

1/4 TEASPOON GROUND CAYENNE
PEPPER

1 CUP FIRMLY PACKED LIGHT
BROWN SUGAR

1/4 CUP BOURBON

2 TABLESPOONS WATER

The Yule celebration brings together family and friends. As we celebrate the return of the Sun God, we also honor each other by gathering together and sharing gifts, food, warmth, and love. Before the festivities begin, you can serve these delicious nuts as appetizers.

Almonds have a milky, mild flavor that blends perfectly with the intensity and warmth of bourbon and the piquant, pine taste of rosemary. If possible, purchase organic almonds in the shell. The shell keeps out the mold, insects, light, and air. When selecting nuts in the shell, look for whole, clean shells with no cracks, blemishes, or holes.

Preheat the oven to 375°F. Place the almonds in a single layer on a baking sheet and toast in the oven until golden and fragrant, about 15 to 20 minutes. Remove and set aside.

In a small bowl, combine the rosemary, cumin, salt, and ground cayenne pepper. In a saucepan, bring the brown sugar, bourbon, and water to a boil over medium heat. Continue boiling for 10 minutes. Add the almonds and stir to coat them completely. Stir in the seasonings and mix well. Transfer the nuts to a buttered baking sheet and separate with a fork while they are still warm. Cool before serving. Store in a container with a tight lid.

LATKES

Serves 4

4 POTATOES

1 APPLE, ANY VARIETY

1 TABLESPOON GRATED ONION

1 LARGE EGG

1/3 CUP ALL-PURPOSE FLOUR

3/4 TEASPOON SALT

1/3 CUP VEGETABLE OIL

SOUR CREAM, APPLESAUCE,
CREAM CHEESE, OR FRUIT
PRESERVE, FOR GARNISH

It is said apples grew abundantly on the mystical island of Avalon, also known as the Isle of Apples. Young women went to the island to receive training in Druid love and guidance in serving the Goddess. Apples can be peeled to divine your future mate (see Apple Scones on page 161 or more details) or to restore a troubled romantic relationship.

On the night of the full moon, gather pictures of you and your loved one, as well as anything that is symbolic of your relationship. Place these items where the moon's luminescent glow can radiate on them. Ground yourself, then light a pink candle. Take the apple to be used for the latkes and cut the fruit lengthwise. Note that the seeds form a heart. Say

Within my soul I hold a great deal of unconditional love.
I possess the ability to empathize with all sides.
I have the strength to overcome all odds.

Leave your objects to bathe in the moonlight all night long.

This particular recipe comes from Andreas Weyermann, who believes to live a harmonious life you must flow with nature.

Peel the potatoes and grate them very finely, which should leave about 3 cups. Squeeze some of the moisture out of the grated potatoes. Peel, core, and finely grate the apple and add it to the potatoes. Add the onion, egg, flour, and salt. Beat until the mixture is well blended.

Pour 1/2 inch of oil into a skillet. When the oil is well heated, drop in the batter by heaping tablespoonsful. Fry until crisp and golden brown on both sides. For crispiest cakes, fry in very hot oil, turning only once. Using moderately warm oil and turning them often leaves the latkes soggy. Remove the pancakes and drain them on paper towels. Serve immediately with sour cream, hot applesauce, cream cheese, or other fruit sauce, if desired.

If you choose to freeze some for later, fry the latkes on each side until they are only slightly golden brown. Drain them on a paper towel. Place the latkes flat in a single layer on an aluminum foil-lined baking sheet. To serve, bake at 425°F for 5 to 10 minutes, until crisp.

Chakra Cranberry Sauce

The Winter Solstice marks the rebirth of the great Sun God, without whom we would not survive. As it is customary to weave a God's Eye during the Summer Solstice, it has become a tradition of the Yuletide celebration as well. For specific instruction, see the recipe for Sun King Pork on page 102. Suggest to your guests that they make a prayer or weave a hope or desire into their God's Eye, using colored yarns that correspond to the colors of the seven chakras, an energetic meditation system adopted by many modern Wiccans. The seven energy centers, or chakras, found within each of us are located along the spine. Each chakra has a representative color and a specific energy or function.

The first chakra, or root chakra, is red and is located at the base of the spine. It grounds us to Mother Earth, is action-oriented, controls our work situations, and affects what we possess in this world. The second chakra is orange, is located in the genitals or womb, and controls reproduction, sexual energy, nurturing, and pleasure. The third chakra is yellow and is known as the solar plexus. Located between the navel and diaphragm, it inhabits the will and affects extreme emotions such as joy and rage. It also affects physical energy levels as well as ability to accomplish goals. The fourth chakra is green and is often called the heart center. Located at the mid-chest, this chakra symbolizes unconditional love and our connection to the Great Mother. Located in the throat, the fifth chakra is blue and presides over the transformation of thought into words, verbal communication, and general creativity. The sixth chakra is purple and often referred to as the Third Eye. Located slightly above the space between the eyebrows, this is the vortex of our inner seeing and where we connect with the Great Spirit. It guides our perceptions and nonverbal communication. The seventh chakra is white and is also known as the crown chakra. Located at top of the head, it directs the light and energy of Divine understanding. Early Christians adapted this chakra by placing halos atop the heads of their saints and angels.

Serves 12

1 CUP WATER

1 CUP GRANULATED SUGAR

1 1/2 CUPS FRESH CRANBERRIES

1 ORANGE, PEELED AND PURÉED

1 APPLE, PEELED, CORED, AND
DICED, ANY VARIETY

1 PEAR, PEELED, CORED, AND
DICED, ANY VARIETY

1 CUP DRIED MIXED FRUIT,
CHOPPED

1 CUP PECANS, CHOPPED

1/2 TEASPOON SALT

1 TEASPOON GROUND CINNAMON

1/2 TEASPOON GROUND NUTMEG

The chakras act like vortexes, each representing a myriad of emotions, concerns, or obstacles that intersect at each location. Suggest to your guests that, given the color or colors they choose to weave into their God's Eye, the corresponding chakra is the what needs their attention most. If a chakra is blocked, it can always be opened; if a chakra is dying, with the right kind of conscious attention, it can bloom again. The state of a chakra is directly contingent upon the level of consciousness the chakra receives. Lead your guests in a meditation through the heart chakra. Ask them to place their consciousness at their heart center. Suggest they enter the heart center by way of another chakra, one with a corresponding color they especially relate to and have featured on the God's Eye. Conclude with a period of silence before gently guiding your friends back to the physical realm.

In a saucepan, boil the water and sugar until the sugar dissolves. Reduce the heat to simmer, and stir in the cranberries, orange, apple, pear, dried fruit, pecans, salt, cinnamon, and nutmeg. Cover, and simmer for 30 minutes, stirring occasionally, until the cranberries burst. Remove from the heat, and let cool to room temperature.

Wheel of the Year Soba and Tofu

Serves 4

2 QUARTS WATER

6 GREEN ONIONS, WHITES AND
GREENS SEPARATED, GREENS CUT
INTO 2-INCH LENGTHS AND
SLICED LENGTHWISE

1 OUNCE FRESH GINGER, PEELED
AND SLICED

3 CLOVES GARLIC, CRUSHED

1 TABLESPOON GRAPESEED OIL

1 (14-OUNCE) PACKAGE
EXTRA-FIRM TOFU, DRAINED
AND PRESSED

SALT AND PEPPER

2 TEASPOONS SOY SAUCE

6 OUNCES SOBA NOODLES

1 HEAD BABY BOK CHOY, TRIMMED
AND THINLY SLICED

4 OUNCES SNOW PEAS, TRIMMED
AND HALVED

1 RED SERRANO CHILE PEPPER

1 TEASPOON BLACK SESAME SEEDS

There are six weeks between each of the Wiccan holidays. Many Wiccan practitioners immerse themselves in the energy of the holiday in the weeks that follow the sabbat day, rather than the weeks that precede it. In other words, from Yule on December 20 to 22 through January, we celebrate the ever-turning Wheel of the Year. We spend this time letting go of the past, honoring the gifts we have received, welcoming the promise of the light, celebrating our loved ones, and recognizing that life is ever evolving and continuous.

This recipe includes soba, a thin Japanese noodle made from buckwheat flour, that is traditionally served on New Year's Eve as a symbol of longevity. New Year (Shogatsu or Oshogatsu) is the most important day on the Japanese calendar. Businesses shut down from January 1 to January 3, and families typically gather for the three-day holiday. It is a time to remember the blessings of the old year and those we hope to receive in the year to come.

As you prepare this dish, give thanks to Ukemochi, the Shinto goddess of food. She is the gentle and generous deity in charge of fertility and nourishment, and the provider of life-sustaining substances.

In a pot with the 2 quarts of water, add the onion whites, ginger, and garlic, and bring to a boil. Cover, and reduce to a simmer, about 25 minutes. In a separate sauté pan warm the oil over medium heat. Slice the tofu in half and season with salt and pepper. Sauté the tofu on all sides, about 15 minutes. Remove the tofu from the pan and set aside to cool; when it's cool enough to handle, slice the cooked tofu into small cubes. Using a slotted spoon, remove the onion, ginger, and garlic from the pot; compost the solids. Bring the broth to a boil; add the soy sauce and soba. Cook the soba for 1 minute or until al dente. Add the boy choy, snow peas, and the chile pepper. Cook until the vegetables are tender-crisp. To serve, place the noodles in a bowl with the broth; top with tofu, onion greens, and sesame seeds.

Note: Store black sesame seeds in the refrigerator to avoid spoiling.

Caraway Breadsticks

3 dozen breadsticks

1 (1/4-OUNCE) PACKAGE ACTIVE DRY YEAST

1 CUP WARM WATER

1 TABLESPOON GRANULATED SUGAR

1/2 TEASPOON GRATED NUTMEG

1 TABLESPOON CHOPPED FRESH SAGE LEAVES

2 TEASPOONS CARAWAY SEEDS

1 1/2 TEASPOONS SALT

1 LARGE EGG

1/4 CUP VEGETABLE SHORTENING

3 1/4 CUPS ALL-PURPOSE FLOUR

Caraway has been used for its culinary and medicinal properties since the Stone Age. Caraway seeds have been found in the remains of Stone Age meals, Egyptian tombs, and ancient caravan stops along the Silk Road. Apples and a dish of caraway seeds were a traditional finish to an Elizabethan feast. Every part of the herb is edible. Caraway is used to relieve colic, balance the digestive system, and sweeten the breath. Caraway is believed to prevent departures and so was included in many love potions. This reason alone sparks many of its uses, both practical and spiritual. The herb has often been sprinkled in with valued possessions in hopes of keeping the goods safe, or at least restraining the thief until the rightful owner returns.

To both attract and maintain love, take a picture of your loved one and place it in a red pouch or cloth filled with caraway seeds and rose petals. Light a pink candle. Say

I now bring thee to me,
By your will do you come.
For love is ours, forever to be.

Blend the yeast and 1/4 cup of the warm water. Let stand for 5 to 10 minutes, until foaming. Mix in the remaining water, sugar, nutmeg, sage, caraway seeds, and salt. Add the egg and the shortening, beating vigorously with a spoon. Sift in the flour, mixing well. Cover and refrigerate for at least 2 hours or overnight.

Divide the chilled dough into 3 dozen small pieces. Roll eight 1-inch pencil-like strips and place them 1 inch apart on a greased baking sheet. Let rise for 1 1/2 to 2 hours.

Preheat the oven to 400°F. Bake the breadsticks for 12 to 15 minutes.

Lambs Wool Apples

Serves 4 to 6

2 CUPS GRANULATED SUGAR

1/2 CUP WATER

1 TEASPOON GRATED NUTMEG

1 TEASPOON GROUND GINGER

1 STICK CINNAMON

1/4 TEASPOON MACE

3 WHOLE ALLSPICE BERRIES

6 LARGE EGGS, SEPARATED

6 CUPS BEER OR ALE

1 CUP BRANDY

1 CUP CREAM SHERRY

6 BAKED APPLES (PAGE 173)

pples are an essential ingredient in this delicious wintertime dish and can also be used to ban negativity from your life. As you prepare this dish, take special care when slicing the apples to visualize yourself cutting away all unfavorable aspects of your nature and life. Take additional apples to your garden, backyard, or other special place of earth where you can dig around a bit. Cut an apple in half crosswise. Draw on the strength and power of the pentagon formed by the seeds. Hold the apple and symbolically pour all your aggravations, ills, and bad habits into the two halves of the cut apple. Alternatively, you can rub the halves on an affected part of the body. Bury the apple during the waning of the moon, thereby banishing, or grounding, all one's ills in the earth. The two-week waning cycle is the time when the moon subsides and life itself seems to be on a diminishing pattern. Therefore it is the perfect occasion for casting out negativity.

Other ceremonial rites that you can perform with the apple include fashioning the wood of the apple tree into charms to promote longevity and taking a libation of apple cider at planting time to ensure a healthy bountiful garden.

In a small saucepan, combine the sugar, water, and spices. Bring to a boil, reduce heat, and simmer for 5 minutes.

In a small bowl, beat the egg whites until they stand in soft peaks. In a separate bowl, beat the egg yolks until slightly thickened and paler yellow. Fold the egg whites and yolks together. Using very large pot, gradually fold the spice mixture into the egg mixture.

In another saucepan, heat the beer, brandy, and sherry. Slowly add the alcohol to the spice and egg mixture. The result should be light and foamy, giving it the name of Lambs Wool Apples. Halve the Baked Apples and float them on top. Serve warm.

Yule Turkey

Turkey has long been a traditional dish during the Winter Solstice. A Yule log is burned to symbolize the return of the Sun God, whose coming marks the beginning of outward expression, in nature and ourselves.

Light your Yule log, sit before it, and try this fire meditation. Through your stomach/solar plexus, direct your consciousness into the flames. Take a deep breath and let the fire reach the extremities of your body, mind, and soul. As you breathe in, the fire expands. As you breathe out, soot and ashes dissolve and recede back into the Mother to be recycled.

Take another deep breath and feel the fire warm your throat. Allow yourself to say what you want to say, for it is your right to speak your truth. The fire is increasing, strengthening, and cleansing your whole being. Listen for any messages. Direct any of the excess heat to go down your arms and legs and out through your hands and feet. See yourself as illuminating light. You may also want to chant this pagan incantation:

> *May the log burn,*
> *May the Wheel turn,*
> *May evil spurn,*
> *May the sun return.*

Your strength and power are ever growing. The meal you have prepared is a reflection of warmth, love, and comfort. It is the true representation of the wealth, abundance, and goodness within you. Everything that you hoped to manifest during this meditation can and will come to you, because you have prepared the fire of action, determination, and success.

Continues on next page

Serves 15 to 20
STUFFING (RECIPE OPPOSITE)

1 TURKEY, 18 TO 22 POUNDS

2 LARGE ORANGES, CUT IN HALF

SALT AND PEPPER

1 CUP UNSALTED BUTTER,
SOFTENED

3 TO 4 TEASPOONS CRUSHED
GARLIC, OR TO TASTE

PAPRIKA

4 TABLESPOONS VEGETABLE OIL

Remove the giblets and neck of the turkey to make the stuffing.

Preheat the oven to 325°F. Wash the turkey well, inside and out. Dry the turkey, inside and out, with paper towels. Squeeze the oranges over the turkey and rub some of the juice on the inside of the turkey cavity. Season the cavity with salt and pepper. Fill the turkey with the stuffing. Close the turkey either by sewing or using trussing skewers. Rub the outside of the turkey with 3/4 cup of the butter and smear the crushed garlic all over it as well. The butter acts as a basting juice during the first half of the cooking time. Season the turkey with salt and pepper and then sprinkle paprika all over it. Drape the turkey with cheesecloth. Place the turkey, breast-side-up, on a rack in a roasting pan. Place the turkey in the oven (see note).

Melt the remaining butter and the vegetable oil in a small saucepan. Lift the cheesecloth every 30 minutes to baste the turkey with the butter mixture. Basting is most important, so do not neglect it! After a while, you can baste with the turkey's own juices. Use a meat thermometer to check for doneness. A turkey is done when the thigh juices run clear yellow when pricked, there are no traces of pinkness, and the drumstick moves easily in its socket. Allow the turkey to stand for 30 minutes. Transfer the stuffing to a bowl and keep warm. Carve the turkey. Serve on a festive platter.

Note: Turkey roasts for about 20 to 30 minutes per pound, so you'll need to cook this one for 9 to 11 hours. Use a meat thermometer and cook it until the thermometer registers the proper temperature for poultry (180° F). Remember to allow plenty of cooking time before you plan to serve the turkey.

STUFFING

This is one of Jamie's family recipes. Her Californio ancestors put this particular combination together. Californios were Spanish rancheros, soldiers, and gentle folk who inhabited California in the late 1700s. Many served in the Spanish army, which helped to colonize the area.

The night before you roast the turkey, toast and lightly butter all of the bread. After you've toasted it, tear off small bite-sized pieces and toss them into a very large skillet. Cook on medium heat and lightly brown the bread pieces until crunchy. Let sit overnight, uncovered.

In the morning, remove the giblets and neck from the turkey and wash them. Boil the giblets and turkey neck in 3 cups of water for 1 to 2 hours in a large saucepan. Add the bouillon cubes. After boiling, save the broth, remove the giblets and neck, and chop them into very small pieces (you may want to use only about half the giblets and neck and give the rest to the dog or cat). Heat the bread crumbs you prepared the night before. Slowly pour about one-third to one-fourth of the turkey giblet broth over the bread, and start to mash the bread mixture with the back of a large spoon. Add the salt, pepper, and sugar. Continue adding broth in small increments, but do not add too much water or it will be soggy; not enough, and you can't mash it! As you blend in the water, add the celery, olives, raisins, giblets, turkey neck, and green onions. Mix it all together and set aside for 10 minutes before you stuff the turkey.

Stuffing

2 LOAVES PRESLICED WHITE BREAD

2 TABLESPOONS BUTTER, SOFTENED

TURKEY GIBLETS AND NECK

1 TO 2 CHICKEN BOUILLON CUBES

SALT AND PEPPER

1 TEASPOON GRANULATED SUGAR

1 CUP CHOPPED CELERY

1 (4-OUNCE) CAN BLACK OLIVES, CHOPPED

1 1/2 CUPS RAISINS

1/4 CUP CHOPPED GREEN ONIONS, ALL PARTS

Stuffed Turkey Burgers

4 burgers

1 POUND GROUND TURKEY

1/2 CUP CHOPPED FRESH THYME

2 TABLESPOONS BREAD CRUMBS

DASH OF SALT

JUICE OF 1/2 LEMON

1/2 CUP CRUMBLED BLUE CHEESE

1/2 TEASPOON LEMON ZEST

The creating of magical charms is the favorite pastime of Yule. As always, the significance you impart into your creation will have a drastic effect on the outcome.

As the Sun God begins His rise in strength and power, we create these amulets, which represent ideas, circumstances, and feelings we would like to see blossom and grow. You need different colors of cloth, and string, ribbon, or yarn, and gemstones, herbs, coins, nuts, or flowers. Use your imagination and possibly a book on gemstones or herbs to balance your intent with the items' properties, adding your love and pure, positive energy. Open your cloth and place inside nuts or seeds for fertility, citrine gemstones or coins for prosperity, rose petals or rose quartz for love, or mistletoe or amethyst for wisdom. Use a green cloth for fertility and prosperity, pink or red for love, or purple for wisdom. Sprinkle a bit of tobacco over your symbolic objects to help tie your wish to Mother Earth. Fold the cloth and tie with the color of string or yarn that corresponds to your wishes.

Alternatively, purchase or make small pouches for your guests. Pass around a box or shell filled with small semiprecious gems or stones with animals or rune symbols painted on them. Invite your guests to take two to three stones or gems. Pass around a box or shell filled with strips of paper, on which you will have written messages ahead of time. These messages can be similar to fortune cookies with inspired meanings or proclamations, such as "The Goddess of Unwavering Faith," "Fertile Abundance," "Compassion," or "Wisdom." In a clockwise circle, ask each of your guests to announce and claim their new title or personal message.

In a large bowl, mix the turkey, thyme, bread crumbs, salt, and lemon juice. Separate the turkey mixture into four parts. Then, form each part into two balls. Flatten each ball into a patty. On top of four of the patties, place 2 tablespoons of the blue cheese and a pinch of the lemon zest. Cover with the remaining four patties and seal the edges by pressing the layers together. This creates four large stuffed burgers. Refrigerate for 1 1/2 hours. Grill to desired doneness.

Tamales de los Martinezo

6 dozen tamales

10 POUNDS PORK ROAST, CUT INTO MEDIUM-SIZE CHUNKS

4 ONIONS

3 WHOLE CLOVES GARLIC

1 TO 2 DRIED ANAHEIM CHILES

1 HEAPING CUP CHILI POWDER

SALT AND PEPPER

1/2 CUP LARD OR CANOLA OIL

2 3/4 CUPS ALL-PURPOSE FLOUR

2 (28-OUNCE) CANS CHILE SAUCE

2 (8-OUNCE) BAGS DRIED CORNHUSKS

10 POUNDS PREMADE MASA

5 (6-OUNCE) CANS WHOLE, PITTED BLACK OLIVES

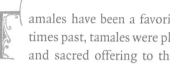amales have been a favorite treat among Latinos for centuries. In times past, tamales were placed on altars by pagans as part of a ritual and sacred offering to the protective deities. The word *tamale* is derived from an Aztec word of the Nahuatl language meaning "wrapped food." Since tamales are often offered as presents during this festive season, this connotation fits in nicely of the Yule tradition of giving wrapped gifts. Tamales are prepared for the largest of the celebrations, including birth, death (on Samhain, known as the Day of the Dead in Mexico), and Yule festivities.

The preparation of this dish is a celebration that can include the entire family. Great variation, versatility, and imagination goes into making tamales, not to mention gossip.

Making tamales is a joyous occasion, one in which you can create a unique experience with your family and friends. You may find that each batch turns out a little different depending on the environment, the stories exchanged, and a combination of the personalities gathered together to cocreate.

To prepare the chili con carne, fill a large pot with 1 inch of water. Add the meat, onions, garlic, chile pods, and 1 tablespoon of the chile powder. Season with salt and pepper. Cook on low heat for 2 1/2 hours. Drain the ingredients. Shred the pork, cutting out any fat.

Mix the lard and flour in a saucepan over low heat. Brown the flour, stirring continually until it is dark beige. Turn off the heat. Slowly stir in the remaining chile powder. Mix until it is an even consistency. Add the chile sauce and 1 can of water (use the chile sauce can). Turn the heat to high and bring to a boil. Use the back of a spatula to mash the mixture until the gravy mixture thickens. Mix in the pork. Decrease heat and simmer for 1 hour.

Recipe continues on next page

Bring some water to boil. Place the cornhusks in a large casserole, cake, or lasagna pan. Pour the boiling water over the cornhusks. Cover with a wet cloth or other light towel. Soak for 20 minutes, until pliable.

Pour the premade masa into a large bowl, leaving the center open. Add 3/4 cup of the sauce, no meat, from the chili con carne. Mix with your hands until fluffy.

Lay a cornhusk flat, with the pointy end away from you. The bottom or longest width of the husk should be approximately 6 to 7 inches wide. You can combine 2 smaller husks, making sure they overlap. Beginning with 1½ inches from the point end, scoop 2 heaping tablespoons of the masa, spreading evenly on each cornhusk. The masa should extend to the bottom and be thick enough so that none of the husk shows through. Place 2 tablespoons of chili con carne in the center of each husk, in an oval shape. Place 1 to 2 olives in the tamale. Roll the tamale lengthwise. Pinch the bottom closed. Fold the pointy end back over the tamale on top of the seam made from rolling the tamale. Seal closed with excess masa.

Pour 2 inches of water in a steamer pot. Stack the tamales, seam side down, in the steamer pot in a circle. Leave the center free. Stack the tamales anywhere from 2 to 4 inches from the top, depending on the size pot you use. Place wet cheesecloth on top of the tamales to keep them from moving. Cover and cook over medium heat. Cooking time varies, depending on the pot you use. If you are using a 2- to 3-gallon pot, cook for 45 minutes to 1 hour; a 4- to 5-gallon pot, cook for 1 to 1½ hours; a 6- to 7-gallon pot, cook for 1½ to 2 hours. The tamales are done when the masa falls freely from the cornhusk.

Note: Some tamale steamer pots are long and rectangular instead of being circular and tall. If you use the rectangular version, stack your tamales standing up against the side. Again, leave the center open.

Yuletide Treats

About 2 dozen cookies

1/2 CUP FIRMLY PACKED LIGHT
BROWN SUGAR

3 TABLESPOONS BUTTER,
SOFTENED

1 LARGE EGG

1 CUP ALL-PURPOSE FLOUR

1/2 TEASPOON BAKING POWDER

1/4 TEASPOON BAKING SODA

1/2 TEASPOON GROUND
CARDAMOM

2 TEASPOONS PUMPKIN OR
APPLE SPICE

RED AND GREEN ICING OR
SPRINKLES, FOR DECORATION

In medieval times, people burned Yule logs to ward off sickness and disease. They then buried some of the ashes, in essence burying their fears and allowing Mother Nature to transform the negative energy into compost, thus bringing forth new life. They saved the rest of the ashes, to sprinkle around the house and grounds for protection, as well as to light the next Yule log.

Light a Yule log (pine or oak is best) to symbolize all that is dying of the old year. Send into the fire those things from which you want to be released. Visualize the rebirth of the sun and the goodness of your spirit as you are fully manifesting into wholeness.

Another tradition associated with the burning of the Yule log was to ensure prosperity for the coming year. Our thoughts about money can either attract money to us or push it away. As you burn your Yule log, make friends with money. See it freely flowing toward you like the energy it is. Being prosperous is your Divine right. The Goddess is the source of all your money and affluence.

Preheat the oven to 375°F. In a large bowl, cream the brown sugar and butter until well blended. Beat the egg separately. Add the egg, beating until well blended. Lightly ladle flour into a measuring cup; level off.

Mix the flour, baking powder, baking soda, and spices in a bowl. Slowly add the flour mixture to the egg mixture, mixing well.

Divide the dough in half. Turn the dough out on a lightly floured surface. Using your hands or a rolling pin, elongate the dough into a log no more than 1 inch wide. Flatten slightly to 1 1/4 inches in diameter.

With a spatula, place the logs 2 to 3 inches apart on an ungreased baking sheet. Dip a nonserrated knife in water. Make 1/4-inch diagonal slashes at 3/4-inch intervals. Either decorate with sprinkles now or with icing later. Bake for 11 to 13 minutes, until set and no longer moist. Cool for 1 minute.

Remove the logs from the baking sheet and place on a wire rack. Cool for 5 minutes. Slice the logs at the scored lines with a serrated knife. Cool completely. Decorate each cookie with decorator icing to resemble a holly leaf and berries.

Dana Dew's Fudge-O-Rama

Makes 5 pounds or 10 dozen 1-inch pieces

1 (5-OUNCE) CAN
EVAPORATED MILK

5 CUPS GRANULATED SUGAR

14 OUNCES MARSHMALLOW WHIP

1/2 CUP UNSALTED BUTTER,
SOFTENED

2 1/2 TEASPOONS VANILLA EXTRACT

2 CUPS WALNUTS, CHOPPED

24 OUNCES SEMISWEET
CHOCOLATE CHIPS

Family bonds and close relationships are particularly important during the Yule season. Whether we are surrounded by friends and relatives, or ones who have passed on, we can always invoke good times by creating traditions that call in love, camaraderie, and happy memories. This easy-to-make recipe is sure to become a favorite family tradition. Have your children help you wrap the fudge pieces using eco-friendly materials like recycled aluminum foil, brown paper grocery bags, old maps, cut-up magazines, scraps of material, or your kids' drawings. Decorate with dried flowers, berries, and leaves or reclaimed ribbons, yarn, twine, or raffia.

This recipe comes from Dana Wardrop, a healer, dark faery, and rocker chick, who makes this recipe every year to commemorate the love she holds for her mother and grandmother.

Grease a 9 by 13-inch baking pan. In a saucepan, mix together the milk and sugar. Bring to a full boil. Continue to boil for five minutes, stirring constantly. Remove from the heat and add the marshmallow whip, butter, vanilla, and nuts. Blend together and immediately pour into the pan. Allow to cool, about 1 hour. When thoroughly cooled, cut into pieces and wrap individually—if you can wait!

Hot Ginger Tea

Serves 4

1 LARGE PIECE FRESH
GINGER, SLICED

1 STICK CINNAMON

SEVERAL LEMON SLICES

SEVERAL WHOLE CLOVES

4 CUPS WATER

3/4 CUP FIRMLY PACKED LIGHT
BROWN SUGAR OR HONEY

Certain customs are so entrenched in Wiccan culture that it is difficult to conceive of ever celebrating without them. Two such traditions are the imbibing of ginger tea and the trimming of a tree at Yule.

Ginger has a heartwarming quality that goes hand in hand with the loving environment created by gathering friends and family for the Yule celebration. In addition to being the perfect antidote for chilly nights, ginger tea is believed to possess the ability to strengthen the lungs and kidneys. The word *yule* derives its meaning from the word "wheel."

The significance of displaying a tree during Yule is connected to the rebirth of the sun. Ancient pagans believed that by bringing in an evergreen tree that grew from the warmth of the sun, they would be symbolically inviting the light into their homes and lives. They decorated the tree with candles as another means of calling in the light. Later they adorned the tree with fruits, nuts, and pinecones, all of which had been nurtured by the invigorating sun.

You may want to consecrate your tree with the four elements before you decorate it. Sprinkle a bit of earth around your tree. Burn incense made from another evergreen, such as pine or rosemary, and allow the smoke to waft through your tree. Light a candle and encircle your tree with it. Lastly, sprinkle the tree with seawater or saltwater.

Press the cloves into the lemon slices. In a saucepan, combine the ginger, cinnamon, lemon slices, and water. Bring to a boil. Reduce the heat, and simmer for 15 to 20 minutes. Sweeten with brown sugar or honey, to taste. Strain and serve hot.

GLÜWEIN

Serves 12 to 14

8 CUPS CABERNET, SAUVIGNON
OR OTHER HEARTY RED WINE

1/2 CUP GRANULATED SUGAR

8 STICKS CINNAMON

4 SLICES ORANGE OR LEMON PEEL

1 TABLESPOON FRESHLY SQUEEZED
LEMON JUICE

2 TABLESPOONS FRESHLY
SQUEEZED ORANGE JUICE

12 WHOLE CLOVES

This spiced wine has been enjoyed in Germany for many generations. It is similar to mulled wine and is served hot during the Yule celebration. Traditionally, the whole family shares the wine, although it is usually watered down for the children.

This ritual begins late in the evening, so the young ones will need to take an afternoon nap. Gather your family around the Tannenbaum (the German name for a Christmas or Yule tree, also known as the sacred tree). Offer each of your family and/or friends a glass of Glüwein, loosely translated meaning "glow wine." You may want to sing carols while you drink the wine. Have Santa visit during the children's nap. Before anyone can tear into the presents, have each person recite a poem or story related to the season. This helps to build up the excitement and reminds everyone of the meaning of the holiday. Themes can relate to the importance of the sun, birth, the light that comes from within, giving unconditionally, or whatever feels right to you. This works best if you ask the children to select a poem or story weeks in advance of the celebration, so they have time to memorize and think about the poem or story they have selected.

Andreas Weyermann donated this family recipe and traditional ritual.

Mix all the ingredients in a large saucepan. Cover and simmer for at least 1 hour.

Note: For children and a more diluted alcohol version, simmer for 30 minutes, covered, then boil, uncovered, for 10 minutes. Some of the alcohol will remain, but much will evaporate using this method.

KITCHEN WITCHERY WITH KIDS

Wicca is a religion that makes sense to kids because it is steeped in love and a respect for all life. Wicca is an everyday spirituality, meaning each time you walk outdoors you are in "church." Practitioners are always surrounded by their teachers—the wind, a bird, a phase of the moon, or the changing leaves of autumn. Wicca does not compartmentalize. Wicca integrates the corporeal and the spiritual, the physical and ephemeral, the seen and the unseen—so that all are seamlessly interwoven.

The gods and goddesses who appear in Wiccan traditions exemplify different aspects of the Divine Source. Their stories serve to make divinity relatable and accessible, rather than esoteric and unapproachable. For example, the Greek deity Ares, god of war, is who we call upon when we need strength and confidence, whereas the Chinese Quan Yin, goddess of compassion, is invoked when we need kindness or empathy. The human-like qualities of these deities demonstrate the Wiccan belief that there is no separation between human and divine: divinity lives within us all.

One of the beautiful and delightful aspects of sharing the Wiccan faith with your children (or nieces, nephews, or grandchildren) is that young people are innately comfortable with the mystery and divinity that surrounds them. When nature provides mystical, magical connections to their feelings and experiences, children accept and embrace those connections without cynicism. It's easy for kids to put their faith in the world of the intangible. As their teachers, all we have to do keep our own minds open to what they already sense instinctively as magical.

Children raised in a Wiccan household will probe and question like all others: it is the natural propensity of all humans to imagine beyond the boundaries of understanding and seek answers. For a child, the discovery of yet another mystery at the end of each question is more exhilarating than exhausting. Sometimes, with frank honesty, and even defiance, our kids may ask us to explain our faith logically. And be fore-warned—in the practice of Wiccan spirituality, there are no "because I said so," answers! We have to be willing to share our ideas, our beliefs, our hopes—even our doubts—with our children. Just as nature is our best teacher and role model, we are the best role models to our children. And when you share your faith with your children, you are offering them a window into your soul.

Wicca is an easily understood approach to spirituality for both young-sters and teenagers. They readily recognize the wisdom inherent in a spirituality that has physical manifestations for its lessons. During the fall season, we teach them it is time to adapt to change—like going to school—as warm weather gives way to brisk breezy days. When winter comes, we show them how to be still and quiet like snow, so that our minds, bodies, and souls can rest. When spring arrives, we awaken like hibernating animals and get busy with useful projects. In summer, we may travel to new places, stretching ourselves like the growing summer-time plants.

By including our kids in the rituals of the seasons at mealtimes, we demonstrate not only to them but also to ourselves that a connection to the Divine does not have to be restricted to holidays or special occasions. In fact, with a nature-based religion, each moment is an opportunity for a spiritual or ethical lesson: whether you are baking bread to share with neighbors in celebration of the autumn harvest or noticing how the first daffodils of spring have beaten back the bitter cold of winter with their cheeriness.

Finally, children offer one of life's greatest gifts: laughter. When you add kids to the mix, you learn to go with the flow and accept the unex-pected. With children in a witch's kitchen, you will learn how to take yourself and your religion lightly. You cannot expect to attend a solemn Samhain ritual if the energy of the room is buoyant with giggling tod-dlers or teenagers. All you can do is remember your intent, add the magical serendipity of the moment, and "mix until thoroughly blended."

This chapter provides more ways to deepen your spiritual practice as you bring your children into the fold of Wicca, or your own earth-centered way of living. The first recipe symbolizes the concept of com-munity, the next one honors the moon, and the eight remaining recipes are organized around the eight sabbats. There is no better way to share your appreciation of the earth's seasonal abundance than by sharing a seasonal meal.

Grandma Gloria's French Bread

2 loaves

1/4 CUP MILK

1 CUP BOILING WATER

1 (2/3-OUNCE) PACKAGE
COMPRESSED FRESH YEAST

1/4 CUP WARM WATER

1 1/2 TABLESPOON MELTED
SHORTENING

1 TABLESPOON GRANULATED
SUGAR

4 CUPS SIFTED ALL-PURPOSE
FLOUR

2 TEASPOONS SALT

2 TEASPOONS SUGAR

Egg Glaze

1 BEATEN EGG WHITE

1 TABLESPOON COLD WATER

his bread can be made with kids as young as two years of age. Baking bread is an excellent way to introduce kids to the warmth and love of the kitchen, and the importance of community. Breaking bread is a kinesthetic, symbolic act of sharing wealth, making peace, developing partnerships, and affirming trust, confidence, and comfort with an individual or group of people. Bake this bread for new neighbors, to celebrate a friendship or new partnership, or to welcome a new season.

This recipe comes from Gloria, a fabulous, gorgeous beacon of light who learned her baking skills from her mother who did everything from scratch and by memory.

In a small pot, bring the milk to a boil. In a separate pot, bring 1 cup of water to a boil, and add the boiling milk. Allow to cool to 85°F. While the milk mixture is cooling, dissolve the yeast in the 1/4 cup of warm water. Allow the dissolved yeast to rest for 10 minutes, then add it to the milk mixture, along with the shortening and 1 tablespoon of the sugar. In a separate bowl, combine the flour, salt, and remaining 2 teaspoons of sugar. Scoop a hole in the center of the dry ingredients, and pour in the liquid mixture. Stir thoroughly, but do not knead. The dough will be soft. Cover with a damp cloth, and set aside in a warm place. Allow the dough to rise for about 2 hours.

Place the risen dough on a lightly floured board and pat into 2 equal oblong shapes. Form each into a French loaf by rolling the dough toward you. Continue rolling, pressing outward with your hands, tapering the ends of the dough until a long thin form is achieved. Place the loaves on a greased baking sheet. Cut diagonal 1/4-inch deep slits across the top of each loaf using a sharp knife. Set the scored loaves aside in a warm place to rise. They should nearly, but not quite double in bulk.

Preheat the oven to 400°F.

On lowest rack in the oven, place a pie pan filled with 1/2-inch boiling water. On the middle rack, bake the bread for 15 minutes. Reduce the heat to 350°F and bake about 30 minutes longer. About 5 minutes before the bread finishes baking, combine the egg white and cold water, and brush the loaves with the egg glaze.

Full Moon Cookies

About 30 cookies

1/2 CUP BUTTER, SOFTENED

1/2 CUP GRANULATED SUGAR

1 TEASPOON VANILLA

2 CUPS ALL-PURPOSE FLOUR

1/2 TEASPOON SALT

bserving the moonrise, as well as its waxing and waning, is an excellent way to involve kids in magic, nature, and science! Because of the moon's orbit around the earth, the moonrise varies from day to day, but will to do so 25 to 45 minutes later each day. During the late summer and early fall, take your kids outdoors at the same time every evening for at least three days. Measure the moon's ascent in the sky with a protractor set on the horizon and the moon. You can also draw the moon to illustrate its growth pattern. A waning moon (one that appears to be getting smaller) is in the shape of a "c." A waxing moon (one that appears to be growing larger) forms a backward "c." When placed together, the backward-facing crescent, a full circle, and the normal crescent form the symbol of the Triple Goddess. Precise moonrise times can be found in your local paper and on the Internet.

As the moon grows in size, the time is ripe to ask for wishes and desires. Make these cookies with your kids during a full moon, and as you stir the batter (in a clockwise direction), share your dreams with them and ask them to share theirs with you.

Preheat the oven to 350°F.

In a bowl, cream the butter and sugar together. Slowly add the remaining ingredients. Roll the batter into small balls and transfer to ungreased cookie sheets. Ask your kids to make moon craters in each cookie using their thumbs. Bake for 10 to 14 minutes.

Note: For a gluten-free alternative, use 1 cup buckwheat and 1 cup garbanzo bean flour instead of all-purpose flour.

Earth Mama Granola Bars

Makes 20 bars

1 CUP HONEY

2/3 CUP NATURAL SMOOTH
PEANUT BUTTER

2 2/3 CUPS ROLLED OATS

1/3 CUP GROUND PECANS OR
WHEAT GERM

1 CUP WHOLE WHEAT FLOUR

1 TEASPOON GROUND CINNAMON

1/2 CUP DRIED CRANBERRIES

1/2 CUP MINI CHOCOLATE CHIPS

1/2 CUP RAW ALMONDS, CHOPPED

1/2 CUP RAW SUNFLOWER SEEDS

These delicious snacks are great for the Imbolc season because they include seeds, an important symbol of the holiday. Celebrated on February 1 or 2, Imbolc marks the beginning of the planting season. The seed represents the spark of inspiration that fuels new ideas and adventures. Hold the sunflower seeds in your hand and teach your children that whatever they plant, it will grow. They cannot expect to plant carrots and harvest apples. Whatever they put out into the world, they will receive back. Even when cooking, their thoughts become ingredients that can affect the outcome.

Additionally, the seed is a symbol of the growing sunlight that chases away the dark of winter. This holiday, also known as Candlemas, or candle mass, represents the time when just a glimmer of light is needed to rejuvenate the soul and spirit. Light a candle either before or after you make these bars. Demonstrate to your children how it only takes a little light to dispel darkness. Suggest that this darkness can be symbolized beyond the long nights or cloudy skies to also represent dark thoughts such as self-doubt, resentment, jealousy, or anger. But when you hold the light, you bring joy and warmth to your immediate surroundings. Tell them that it takes only one person (and there are many examples in history, your neighborhood, and family) can hold the light of positive thoughts and lead the way for others to follow.

Preheat the oven to 350°F.

In a small pan, warm the honey slightly. In a bowl, add the peanut butter and the warmed honey and stir to combine. Add the oats, ground pecans, flour, and cinnamon. Stir in the remaining ingredients. Place the dough in a greased 9 by 13-inch baking pan, pressing down firmly it is evenly distributed. Bake for 15 minutes, until the edges begin to brown. Remove from oven and immediately cut into 20 bars. Then allow to cool completely before serving.

Ostara Rolls

12 rolls

1½ CUPS THAI PEANUT SAUCE

1 (1½-INCH) PIECE FRESH
GINGER ROOT, MINCED

2 CLOVES GARLIC, MINCED

2 TEASPOONS SOY SAUCE

1 POUND BONELESS, SKINLESS
CHICKEN BREASTS, CUT IN HALF,
THEN CUT INTO 1-INCH PIECES

2 TABLESPOONS PEANUT OIL

¼ CUP FRESH SNOW PEA PODS

1½ CUPS BEAN SPROUTS

4 GREEN ONIONS, ALL PARTS,
CHOPPED

2 CUPS WATERCRESS, CHOPPED

¼ CUP FRESH CILANTRO, CHOPPED

2 LARGE CARROTS, PEELED, AND
SHAVED INTO THIN STRIPS

12 SPRING ROLL WRAPPERS

 he word *Ostara* originates from Eostre, the Germanic Goddess of Spring, and follows a similar evolution as the word *Easter*, which is always celebrated on the first Sunday that follows the first full moon after the Spring Equinox.

As you make this recipe, have your children pretend they are different members of nature's interconnected community. One child can be a beaver, another child can be a frog living on the riverbank, another child can be a fish in the river, and another an eagle nesting high above the river. Explain that if the beaver goes away, everyone goes hungry: the frog has no pond in which to lay her eggs because the river wasn't dammed by the beaver; the fish who eat the tadpoles go hungry; the eagle who eats the fish goes hungry. So the beaver (a keystone species) and his activities are essential to the health of his environment and well-being of his neighbors.

In a bowl, combine 1 cup of the peanut sauce with the ginger, garlic, and 1 teaspoon of the soy sauce. Add the chicken pieces, and mix until the chicken is coated. Marinate in the refrigerator for 30 minutes. Heat 1 tablespoon of the peanut oil in a wok or skillet over medium heat. Cook the snow peas, bean sprouts, and green onion in the oil until heated but still crisp, 3 to 4 minutes. Transfer to a large bowl. Add the watercress and cilantro and combine. Add the shaved carrot. Drizzle the remaining 1 teaspoon of soy sauce into the watercress mixture; toss to coat. Add 1 tablespoon of the oil to the wok or skillet. Add the marinated chicken and cook until the flesh is no longer pink, about 10 minutes.

Fill a large bowl with hot water. Dip a wrapper into the water for about 2 seconds. Remove from the water and immediately fill with 2 tablespoonfuls of the chicken and 1 tablespoonful of the watercress mixture. Fold over the opposite ends of the wrapper to overlap the filling. Then bring the bottom of the wrapper over the top of the filling, and roll. Repeat with the remaining wrappers and filling. Serve with remaining 1 cup of peanut sauce for dipping.

Note: You can also make these Ostara Rolls without the chicken and simply use more vegetables.

Cheesey Toast

Serves 4

2 TABLESPOONS SHREDDED
CHEDDAR CHEESE

1 TABLESPOON SHREDDED
MONTEREY JACK CHEESE

2 TABLESPOONS GRATED
PARMESAN CHEESE

1/2 TEASPOON FRESH CHOPPED
PARSLEY

1/2 TEASPOON FRESH CHOPPED
OREGANO

1/2 TEASPOON FRESH CHOPPED
BASIL,

1/2 TEASPOON GREEN ONION,
WHITE PART ONLY, MINCED

2 TABLESPOONS BUTTER

1/2 CLOVE GARLIC, PRESSED

1/4 LOAF FRENCH BREAD

This recipe is included to commemorate Lammas, the first of three harvest holidays. It is a moment to remember to be grateful, bless the tools of our trade, celebrate the fruits of our labor, and honor our talents and our achievements.

Have your kids write on a piece of paper all the accomplishments that they're proudest of. Discuss and list the qualities or characteristics (or tools of their trade) they needed into order to realize their goals. What other rewards (or fruits of their labor) have come from their achievements? Have they inspired others? Are they motivated to try harder next time? Has their confidence grown? Have they made a new friendship? Abolished an old fear? Then have the children repeat:

I am grateful for what I accomplished on this day
And good qualities that assist me along the way.
I am thankful that the good I do can help others
Doing my best shines lights on my sisters and brothers.

Preheat the oven to 450°F.

In a bowl, mix the cheeses, herbs, and green onion. In a large skillet, melt the butter over low heat. Add the garlic. Place the quarter loaf of French bread face down in the melted butter. Brush the back of the loaf with butter from the pan. Place the butter-coated bread face up on a cookie sheet and spread with the cheese mixture. Heat for 8 to 10 minutes in the oven, until the edges begin to brown. If you like it crispier, toast quickly for 1 to 2 minutes under the broiler or in a preheated toaster oven.

CHERRY SCONES

16 scones

2 1/4 CUPS ALL-PURPOSE FLOUR

1/2 CUP OATMEAL

1/3 CUP GRANULATED SUGAR
PLUS 1 TABLESPOON, DIVIDED

2 TEASPOONS BAKING POWDER

1/2 TEASPOON BAKING SODA

1/2 TEASPOON GROUND CINNAMON

1/4 TEASPOON SALT

1/4 CUP COLD UNSALTED BUTTER,
CUT INTO SMALL PIECES

3/4 CUP DRIED TART CHERRIES,
FINELY CHOPPED

1/2 CUP LOWFAT BUTTERMILK

3 LARGE EGGS

1 TABLESPOON WATER

As we dance around the May Pole during the Beltane holiday, we are rejoicing in anticipation of a bountiful harvest. The May Pole, traditionally a tree cut from the forest on April 30, represents the male energy of light and action. It is straight as a sword, and sends a bold, straightforward message of fertility. The ribbons attached to the May Pole dance in the wind and their flexibility represents the kinetic female energy—harbinger of growth. The way the dancing ribbons are woven around the steadfast pole creates a uniquely individual pattern—just like your child is a unique individual. The May Pole dance is a reenactment of faith—faith that the ribbon-bedecked pole will represent a plentiful harvest coming in a few months' time.

Faith is the bridge that all miracles travel upon. It is the power that says yes to what is not yet seen. Belief pushes and prods the desires of our hearts along the route from the invisible world of our imagination to the visible world we live in.

In a mixing bowl, combine the dry ingredients. Using a mixer on low speed, cut in the butter. until the mixture resembles coarse meal. Stir in the dried cherries. In a separate bowl, whisk together the buttermilk and 2 of the eggs. Add the liquid mixture to dry mixture, stirring just until moist. The dough will be soft and sticky. Allow the dough to rest for 10 minutes.

Preheat the oven to 400°F.

Flour a board or work surface. Turn out the dough and knead 2 to 3 times. The dough will be very soft. Divide the dough in half. Roll each half into a 5-inch circle, about 3/4-inch thick. Using a sharp knife, cut each round into 8 pie-shaped wedges. Using a metal spatula, carefully transfer the wedges onto a baking sheet, arranging them so they do not touch, at least 1 1/2 inches apart. In a small bowl, whisk the remaining egg with the 1 tablespoon of water to make the egg wash. Brush a very light coat of the egg wash atop each scone; sprinkle the scones with the remaining tablespoon of sugar. Bake for about 13 minutes, or until the tops are lightly browned and the insides fully baked. The scones will be firm to the touch. Serve warm.

Summertime Garden Pizza

2 twelve-inch pizzas

Dough

1 (1/4-OUNCE) PACKAGE ACTIVE
DRY YEAST

1 CUP WARM WATER

3 CUPS ALL-PURPOSE FLOUR
PLUS ADDITIONAL AS NEEDED,
FOR KNEADING

2 TABLESPOONS EXTRA VIRGIN
OLIVE OIL

1 1/2 TEASPOONS SALT

The mix of toppings for this pizza is a proud display of summer's lavishly diverse abundance. You can use pizza preparation time to show your children how important diversity is—diversity in nature and among people. Like each edible ingredient that goes into the pizza, all children have their own unique "flavor signature."

Ask each child pretend to be one of the plants—an herb or vegetable—that will be represented on the pizza. Ask them what happens as they grow. For example, how does the tomato feel as it turns from green to yellow to red? What is it like for a basil leaf to unfold in the sun? Are the mushrooms comfy in the cool, damp soil? What does the olive experience as it hangs from its tree branch? The broccoli? The bell peppers? Share with your children how diverse environments and experiences and individuals will enrich their lives in the same way that a diversity of ingredients will combine to create a scrumptious pizza!

Place the yeast in a large mixing bowl. Add the water and stir with a long-handled wooden spoon, until the yeast is dissolved. After a few minutes, bubbles should appear on the surface of the yeast mixture, indicating the yeast is working. Add the flour, 1 tablespoon of the oil, and the salt, and stir well to combine. Continue stirring until the dough pulls away from the sides of the bowl. Place the dough on a lightly floured surface. Knead until it forms a smooth, elastic ball, about 3 to 5 minutes.

Grease a large bowl with 1 tablepoon of the remaining oil. Place the dough in the bowl, turning it to coat. Cover with a damp cloth or plastic wrap. Place in a warm, draft-free place and let rise until doubled in size, about 1 to 2 hours.

Continues on next page

===

Sauce

2 TABLESPOONS OLIVE OIL

1¹/₂ CUPS CHOPPED YELLOW ONION

1 TEASPOON MINCED GARLIC

¹/₂ TEASPOON SALT

2 TEASPOONS FRESH CHOPPED
BASIL

1 TEASPOON FRESH CHOPPED
OREGANO

¹/₈ TEASPOON FRESHLY GROUND
BLACK PEPPER

2 (28-OUNCE) CANS WHOLE
PEELED TOMATOES

2 (15-OUNCE) CANS TOMATO SAUCE

3 TABLESPOONS TOMATO PASTE

2 CUPS WATER

1 TEASPOON GRANULATED SUGAR

Toppings

¹/₂ CUP MOZZARELLA CHEESE,
GRATED

¹/₂ CUP MONTEREY JACK CHEESE,
GRATED

¹/₂ CUP PARMESAN CHEESE, GRATED

¹/₂ CUP BROCCOLI, DICED

¹/₂ CUP RED OR GREEN BELL
PEPPERS, SLICED

¹/₂ CUP MUSHROOMS , SLICED

While the dough is rising, heat the olive oil in a large, heavy pot over medium heat. Add the onions, garlic, salt, basil, oregano, and pepper, and cook, stirring, until soft, about 5 minutes. Place the tomatoes in a large mixing bowl and squish with a spoon or your hands (or your kids' hands—they'll love doing this!) to break them into small pieces. Add the tomatoes, tomato sauce, tomato paste, water, and sugar to the pot with the onion mixture, and stir well. Bring to a simmer over medium-high heat. Lower the heat to medium-low and simmer, uncovered, for 45 minutes, stirring occasionally with a long-handled wooden spoon.

Place the oven rack in the lowest position in the oven and preheat the oven to 500°F.

Lightly grease two baking sheets. Set aside. Divide the dough into two portions and shape into two smooth balls. Pat one dough ball into a flat round, about 6 inches in diameter, onto a prepared baking sheet. Repeat with the second ball of dough. Allow both to rest for 10 minutes. With your fingertips, press each dough round into a thinner, 12-inch round, or roll with a rolling pin.

Spoon the sauce onto the dough round. Using the back of a spoon, spread the sauce to within 1 inch of the edge of the crust. Sprinkle the cheese evenly on top. Add the vegetables. Bake on the lowest rack of the oven until the cheese is bubbly and golden brown, about 10 to 12 minutes.

Autumn Awesome Apple Pie

1 twelve-inch pie

Filling

3 TO 5 APPLES (YOUR
FAVORITE VARIETY)

2 BARTLETT PEARS

2 1/2 TABLESPOONS CINNAMON

1/4 CUP LEMON JUICE, OR
MIX LIME, TANGERINE, AND
ORANGE JUICE FOR A SUBTLY
DIFFERENT FLAVOR

1 CUP RAISINS OR DRIED
CRANBERRIES, OR BOTH

1/2 CUP HONEY

1/2 CUP LIGHT BROWN SUGAR

4 CLOVES, WHOLE OR GROUND

Crust

3 CUPS WHOLE WHEAT FLOUR

1/2 CUP WATER

1/4 CUP CHILLED BUTTER,
SHAVED OR GRATED

Autumn signifies a time of change. Some plants and insects go dormant, existing in suspended animation through the winter months until spring temperatures "wake" them. Some animals migrate hundreds, even thousands of miles to gorge on summer's bounty, building up stores of fat for the cold season ahead when forage is meager. Some mammals hibernate, sleeping through the winter, living off their fat reserves while tucked away in a warm log or burrow.

Apples change from bud to blossom to fruit and are transformed into this delicious pie. Any way you look at it, flora and fauna provide awesome examples of how to adapt to life's endless seasonal changes.

This pie was created by Dr. Jeep Pagel, a zealous raptor ecologist whose passion for conservation of species and open spaces is absolutely contagious.

Preheat the oven to 350°F.

Slice the apples and pears into thin chunks and place in a large bowl. Add the cinnamon, lemon juice, raisins, honey, and brown sugar. Using a knife, mix the ingredients, chopping the apples and pears into smaller 1-inch pieces as you mix. Set aside. In a separate bowl, mix together the flour, water, and butter. Knead the dough by squeezing it through your fingers. Roll into a large ball, and divide into two portions, making one portion larger with 2/3 of the dough, and the other portion smaller with the remaining 1/3 (for the top crust). Using a well-floured rolling pin, roll out the larger dough ball into a 1/4-inch-thick circle. Grease a twelve-inch pie pan and place crust in the pan. Spoon the filling into the crust. Roll out the second dough ball into a smaller 1/4-inch-thick circle. Using your fingers, wet the edge of the filled crust with a little water. Then cover the filled pie with the top crust. Pinch the edges together to seal the crusts together. Trim the excess dough from the rim of the pan. Poke air holes in top crust. Cut or grate 2 tablespoons of butter into smaller pieces and spread over the crust. Bake for 50 minutes to 1 hour, or until a sharp knife inserted into the pie indicates the apples are soft. Remove from the oven and let stand for 15 minutes or more as you savor the smell of freshly baked apples and cinnamon. Enjoy with ice cream and cider.

Magickal Roasted Pumpkin Pasta

The quintessential food for Samhain is pumpkin, not only because it is a widely recognized symbol for Halloween, but also because it's the fruit we are harvesting at this time. Samhain is to a year, what twilight is to a day. It is the place in between, where the noise of summer meets the silence of winter. In this borderland, magick is created. Magick spelled with a "k" is not about magic tricks, like pulling a bunny out of a hat. The "g" points to the ground, the vortex triangle that points to the earth and usually represents yin, female, or resting energy. The "k" reaches for the sky, where ideas are born, similar to the apex triangle that is typically considered yang, male, or active energy. The overlapping vortex and apex triangles create a symbol, known as the Star of David. The intersection of form and material or thought and spirit is where magick happens.

Imagine with your little kitchen helpers a place in the woods where two paths intersect. Animals of all kinds cross this way. Travelers from far and wide meet at this place. Here, anything can happen. Visualize a cloaked figure on horseback who rides up to greet your kids. He wants to hear their deepest secrets and dearest wishes. He will carry them to magickal places where they will find flight and return as dreams come true. Have your children tell the dark rider their wishes and dreams. Encourage them to tell him how they'll feel when their dearest desires are manifested. Have them speak all these details into the pumpkin, then tell your children to let them go.

Explain that when we make a wish we must release it to allow it to come back to us. We must tell ourselves that the Universe will go to work on it as soon as we speak our aspiration. To revisit and concentrate on not having our desires met is akin to digging up a seed over and over again to see if it's taken root! Make a wish and let it go.

This recipe comes to us from Mama Mango, a garden goddess who now nurtures her two magikal children and tends her biodynamic garden in southern California.

Serves 8

========

1 MEDIUM-SIZED SUGAR PUMPKIN

3 CLOVES OF GARLIC, CRUSHED

2 TO 3 TABLESPOONS OLIVE OIL

1 TEASPOON SEA SALT

1 TEASPOON BLACK PEPPER

1 TEASPOON TAMARI SAUCE
(OPTIONAL)

5 FRESH BAY LEAVES

8 TO 10 FRESH SAGE LEAVES

16 OUNCES SPAGHETTI OR
TAGLIATELLE PASTA

2 TABLESPOONS BUTTER

SALT AND PEPPER

1/2 CUP PARMESAN OR GRANA
PADANO CHEESE, GRATED

Preheat the oven to 425°F.

Peel the pumpkin. Remove seeds to save for roasting or planting. Cut the pumpkin into rough cubes. Place the pumpkin and garlic on a baking sheet, drizzle with plenty of olive oil, and toss to coat. Sprinkle with the salt, pepper, and tamari, turning the pumpkin pieces to coat. Add the bay leaves. Roast the pumpkin in the oven for about 15 to 20 minutes, or until the pumpkin has softened, caramelized, and is slightly crispy around the edges.

While the pumpkin is roasting, boil water for the spaghetti. Cook the spaghetti, and drain. Set aside.

Melt the butter in a large frying pan. Sauté the sage leaves for 2 to 3 minutes, taking care not the burn the butter. (Do not substitute dried sage for fresh leaves.) Add salt and pepper to taste.

Remove the pumpkin from the oven, and remove the bay leaves from the baking sheet. Add the cooked pumpkin mixture to the frying pan. Gently turn the pumpkin over in the butter and sage, taking care not to break up the pieces in the process. Add the spaghetti to the frying pan. Carefully toss the ingredients together and serve with Parmesan or Grana Padano cheese.

No Leftovers Lentil–Cauliflower Soup

Serves 8

2 TABLESPOONS OLIVE OIL

4 CARROTS, SLICED

4 CELERY STALKS, SLICED

1 YELLOW ONION, CHOPPED FINE

4 SMALL OR 2 LARGE RED
POTATOES, DICED

1 TO 2 TEASPOONS SALT

1/8 TEASPOON PEPPER

1 TEASPOON CORIANDER

1 TEASPOON TURMERIC

1 TEASPOON CUMIN

8 CUPS WATER OR VEGETABLE
BROTH, OR 4 CUPS OF EACH

1 CUP GREEN LENTILS

1 HEAD CAULIFLOWER, CHOPPED
INTO SMALL PIECES

1/4 CUP TOMATO SAUCE

2 BAY LEAVES

The warming quality of this soup is perfect for the Winter Solstice, the longest, darkest night of the year. There is so much going on at this holiday, the chaos can be unnerving to everyone—young and old. The Winter Solstice is a perfect holiday to help your children realize their capacity to just "go with the flow," and though they may lose one thing, certainly they will gain another. Remind little ones they must give up standing in order to sit down. And, conversely, they must be willing to lose their lap when they stand up!

Yuletide commemorates and venerates hope and renewal by putting its faith in the Wheel of Life, as in the turning, always moving, always changing. In fact, the word *yule* means "wheel." Round holiday wreaths symbolize the circular nature of life, which includes death and rebirth. The lights we put on our holiday trees represent the promise of the gradually growing light of the sun. The tree itself represents the greenness that is returning to the earth. Remind your children that every winter gives way to spring, and every spring evolves into summer, and every summer transforms into fall, and every fall returns to winter. When, of course, it begins all over again. Nothing is ever lost, it only changes form.

This recipe was donated by Kristen Stirbu, a mother of five children, who uses her time in the kitchen to learn and teach others about the healing power of whole foods.

In a large sauté pan, heat the olive oil. Add the carrots, celery, onion, and potatoes and sauté. Add the salt, pepper, coriander, turmeric, and cumin. Add the water and the lentils. Cook over low heat for at least 1 hour. The longer it cooks, the better the flavors will meld together. Add the cauliflower and the tomato sauce, and cook about 20 minutes more. Serve with bread or cheese toast.

BIBLIOGRAPHY

Bethards, Betty, *The Dream Book: Symbols for Self-Understanding*. Rockport, MA: Element, 1995.

Black, Maggie. *The Medieval Cookbook*. New York: Thames and Hudson, Inc., 1992.

Cahill, Sedonia, and Joshua Halpern. *The Ceremonial Circle: Practice, Ritual, and Renewal for Personal and Community Healing*. San Francisco, CA: HarperSanFrancisco, 1990.

Campbell, Joseph. *Myths to Live By*. New York: Bantam Books, 1972.

Cosman, Madeleine Pelner. *Fabulous Feasts: Medieval Cookery and Ceremony*. New York: George Braziller, 1976.

Driver, Christopher, and Michelle Berriedale-Johnson. *Pepys at Table: Seventeenth Century Recipes for the Modern Cook*. Berkeley: University of California Press, 1984.

Dunwich, Gerina. *Wicca Craft: The Modern Witch's Book of Herbs, Magick, and Dreams*. Secaucus, NJ: Citadel Press Books, 1997.

Foundation for Inner Peace. *A Course in Miracles*. 2nd ed. New York: Viking Press, 1996.

Gibran, Khalil. *The Prophet*. New York: Knopf, 1969.

Graves, Robert. *The White Goddess*. New York: Farrar, Straus, Giroux, 1948.

Grimassi, Raven. *Ways of the Strega—Italian Witchcraft: Its Lore, Magick, and Spells*. St. Paul, MN: Llewellyn Publications, 1995.

Henisch, Bridget Ann. *Fast and Feast: Food in Medieval Society*. University Park and London: Pennsylvania State University Press, 1976.

Hieatt, Constance B., Brenda Hosington, and Sharon Butler, eds. *Pleyn Delit: Medieval Cookery for Modern Cooks*. 2nd ed. Toronto: University of Toronto Press, 1996.

Holmes, Urban Tigner, Jr. *Daily Living in the Twelfth Century: Based on the Observations of Alexander Neckham in London and Paris*. Reprint. Madison, WI: The University of Wisconsin Press, 1980.

Jensen, M.D., Bernard, *Foods That Heal: A Guide to Understanding and Using the Healing Powers of Natural Foods*. Garden City Park, NY: Avery Publishing Group, 1988.

Jung, Carl. *Man and His Symbols*. Garden City, NY: Doubleday, 1964.

Kenyon, Sherrilyn. *The Writer's Guide to Everyday Life in the Middle Ages: The British Isles, 500 to 1500*. Cincinnati, OH: Writer's Digest Books, 1995.

Kowalchik, Claire, and William H. Hylton. *Rodale's Illustrated Encyclopedia of Herbs*. Emmaus, PA: Rodale Press, 1987.

Kruger, Anna. *An Illustrated Guide to Herbs: Their Medicine and Magic*. Surrey, Great Britain: Dragon's World Ltd., 1993.

McCoy, Edain. *The Sabbats: A New Approach to Living the Old Ways*. St. Paul, MN: Llewellyn Publications, 1994.

McIntire, Virginia Allen. *Color Energy: Meditation for Mind/Body/Spirit*. Beverly Hills, CA: Virginia Allen McIntire, Ph.D., 1986.

Mennell, Stephen. *All Manners of Food: Eating and Taste in England and France from the Middle Ages to the Present*. Oxford, UK: Basil Blackwell, 1985.

Mességué, Maurice. *Health Secrets of Plants and Herbs*. New York: William Morrow, 1975.

Miller, Mark, Stephen Pyles, and John Sedlar. *Tamales*. New York: Macmillan, 1997.

Ody, Penelope. *The Complete Medicinal Herbal*. London: Dorling Kindersley, 1993.

Roberts, Morgan J. *The Norse Gods and Heroes*. New York: Metro Books, 1995.

Rolleston, T. W. *Celtic Myths and Legends*. New York: Dover Publications, 1990.

Sams, Jamie, and David Carson. *Medicine Cards*. Santa Fe, NM: Bear & Co., 1988.

Scully, Terrence. *The Art of Cookery in the Middle Ages*. Woodbridge, UK: Boydell Press, 1995.

Starhawk. *Spiral Dance: A Rebirth of the Ancient Religion of the Great Goddess*. San Francisco, CA: HarperSanFrancisco, 1979.

Starhawk, Diane Baker, and Anne Hill. *Circle Round: Raising Children in Goddess Tradition*. New York: Bantam Doubleday Dell, 1998.

Waldherr, Kris. *The Book of Goddesses*. Hillsboro, OR: Beyond Words Publishing, 1995.

Weiss, Gaea, and Shandor. *Growing and Using the Healing Herbs*. Emmaus, PA: Wings Books, 1985.

Williamson, Darcy, and Lisa Railsback. *Cooking with Spirit: North American Indian Food and Fact*. Bend, OR: Maverick Publications, 1993.

Williamson, Marianne. *A Woman's Worth*. New York: Random House, 1993.

INDEX

Metric Conversion Chart

LENGTH

INCH	METRIC
1/4 inch	6 mm
1/2 inch	1.25 cm
3/4 inch	2 cm
1 inch	2.5 cm
6 inches (1/2 foot)	15 cm
12 inches (1 foot)	30 cm

TEMPERATURE

FAHRENHEIT	CELSIUS/GAS MARK
250°F	120°C/gas mark 1/2
275°F	135°C/gas mark 1
300°F	150°C/gas mark 2
325°F	160°C/gas mark 3
350°F	180 or 175°C/gas mark 4
375°F	190°C/gas mark 5
400°F	200°C/gas mark 6
425°F	220°C/gas mark 7
450°F	230°C/gas mark 8
475°F	245°C/gas mark 9
500°F	260°C

VOLUME

U.S.	IMPERIAL	METRIC
1 tablespoon	1/2 fl oz	15 ml
2 tablespoons	1 fl oz	30 ml
1/4 cup	2 fl oz	60 ml
1/3 cup	3 fl oz	90 ml
1/2 cup	4 fl oz	120 ml
2/3 cup	5 fl oz (1/4 pint)	150 ml
3/4 cup	6 fl oz	180 ml
1 cup	8 fl oz (1/3 pint)	240 ml
1 1/4 cups	10 fl oz (1/2 pint)	300 ml
2 cups (1 pint)	16 fl oz (2/3 pint)	480 ml
2 1/2 cups	20 fl oz (1 pint)	600 ml
1 quart	32 fl oz (1 2/3 pint)	1 l

WEIGHT

U.S./IMPERIAL	METRIC
1/2 oz	15 g
1 oz	30 g
2 oz	60 g
1/4 lb	115 g
1/3 lb	150 g
1/2 lb	225 g
3/4 lb	350 g
1 lb	450 g